Say It Right in
ITALIAN

Second Edition

Easily Pronounced Language Systems

Clyde Peters, Author

New York   Chicago   San Francisco   Lisbon   London   Madrid   Mexico City
Milan   New Delhi   San Juan   Seoul   Singapore   Sydney   Toronto

The McGraw·Hill Companies

1 2 3 4 5 6 7 8 9 10 11 12 13 14 15   QFR/QFR   1 9 8 7 6 5 4 3 2 1

ISBN   978-0-07-176775-0
MHID   0-07-176775-4

Library of Congress Cataloging-in-Publication Data

Say it right in Italian / Easily Pronounced Language Systems — 2nd ed.
      p.   cm. — (Say it right)
   Includes index.
   Text in English and Italian.
   ISBN 978-0-07-176775-0 (alk. paper)
    1. Italian language—Pronunciation by foreign speakers.   2. Italian language — Spoken Italian.   3. Italian language — Conversation and phrase books —English.   I. Easily Pronounced Language Systems.   II. Clyde E. Peters, Author.

   PC1137.S39   2011
   458.3′421—dc22   2011011955

Clyde Peters, author
Luc Nisset, illustrations
Betty Chapman, EPLS contributor, www.isayitright.com
Priscilla Leal Bailey, senior series editor
Lucia Colazio, Italian language consultant

Also available:
Say It Right in Chinese, Second Edition
Say It Right in French, Second Edition
Say It Right in Spanish, Second Edition

For more titles and apps, see page 179.

Perfect your pronunciation by listening to sample phrases from this book. Go to www.audiostudyplayer.com, launch the Study Player, and then select: Italian>For Travel>Say It Right in Italian.

McGraw-Hill books are available at special quantity discounts to use as premiums and sales promotions or for use in corporate training programs. To contact a representative, please e-mail us at bulksales@mcgraw-hill.com.

This book is printed on acid-free paper.

CONTENTS

INTRODUCTION

The SAY IT RIGHT FOREIGN LANGUAGE PHRASE BOOK SERIES has been developed with the conviction that learning to speak a foreign language should be fun and easy!

All SAY IT RIGHT phrase books feature the EPLS Vowel Symbol System, a revolutionary phonetic system that stresses consistency, clarity, and above all, simplicity!

Since this unique phonetic system is used in all SAY IT RIGHT phrase books, you only have to learn the VOWEL SYMBOL SYSTEM ONCE!

The SAY IT RIGHT series uses the easiest phrases possible for English speakers to pronounce and is designed to reflect how foreign languages are used by native speakers.

You will be amazed at how confidence in your pronunciation leads to an eagerness to talk to other people in their own language.

Whether you want to learn a new language for travel, education, business, study, or personal enrichment, SAY IT RIGHT phrase books offer a simple and effective method of pronunciation and communication.

PRONUNCIATION GUIDE

Most English speakers are familiar with the Italian word **Pizza**. This is how the correct pronunciation is represented in the EPLS Vowel Symbol System.

All Italian vowel sounds are assigned a specific non-changing symbol.

When these symbols are used in conjunction with consonants and read normally, pronunciation of even the most difficult foreign word becomes incredibly EASY.

On the following page are all the EPLS Vowel Symbols used in this book. They are EASY to LEARN since their sounds are familiar. Beneath each symbol are three English words which contain the sound of the symbol.

Practice pronouncing the words under each symbol until you mentally associate the correct vowel sound with the correct symbol. Most symbols are pronounced the way they look!

THE SAME BASIC SYMBOLS ARE USED IN ALL SAY IT RIGHT PHRASE BOOKS!

EPLS VOWEL SYMBOL SYSTEM

(A)
Ace
Bake
Safe

(EE)
See
Feet
Meet

(I)
Ice
Kite
Pie

(O)
Oak
Cold
Sold

(OO)
Cool
Pool
Too

(ĕ)
Men
Red
Bed

(ah)
Calm
Hot
Off

(OW)
Cow
How
Now

(OY)
Toy
Boy
Joy

EPLS CONSONANTS

Consonants are letters like **T**, **D**, and **K**. They are easy to recognize and their pronunciation seldom changes. The following EPLS pronunciation guide letters represent some unique Italian consonant sounds.

Ŗ	Represents a slightly rolled **r** sound.
Ŗ̧	Represents a strongly rolled **r** sound.
TS	Represents the letter **z** in Italian. Pronounce the word hi**ts** without the hi or simply say pi**zz**a! Listen closely to a native speaker to master this sound.
KY	Pronounce like the **c** in **c**ute.
CH	Pronounce like the **ch** in **ch**air.

PRONUNCIATION TIPS

- Each pronunciation guide word is broken into syllables. Read each word slowly, one syllable at a time, increasing speed as you become more familiar with the system.

- In Italian it is important to emphasize certain syllables. This mark (´) over the syllable reminds you to stress that syllable.

- This phrase book provides a means to speak and be understood in Italian. **To perfect your Italian accent you must listen closely to Italian speakers and adjust your speech accordingly.**

- The pronunciation and word choices in this book were chosen for their simplicity and effectiveness.

- **PF** or **PPC** are abbreviations for **per favore** or **per piacere** which means "please" in Italian. You will see these abbreviations throughout the book.

ICONS USED IN
THIS BOOK

KEY WORDS

You will find this icon at the beginning of chapters indicating key words relating to chapter content. These are important words to become familiar with.

PHRASEMAKER

The Phrasemaker icon provides the traveler with a choice of phrases that allows the user to make his or her own sentences.

Say It Right in ITALIAN

ESSENTIAL WORDS AND PHRASES

Here are some basic words and phrases that will help you express your needs and feelings in **Italian**.

Hello

Buon giorno

BWON JOR-NO

How are you?

Come sta?

KO-ME STah

Fine / Very well

Molto bene

MOL-TO BE-NE

And you?

E lei?

E LE-EE

Good-bye

Arrivederci

ah-REE-VE-DER-CHEE

Good morning

Buon giorno

BWON JOB-NO

Good evening

Buona sera

BWO-Nah SĕB-Bah

Good night

Buona notte

BWO-Nah NOT-Tĕ

Mr.

Signor

SEEN-YOB

Mrs.

Signora

SEEN-YO-Bah

Miss

Signorina

SEEN-YO-BEE-Nah

Yes

Sí

SEE

No

No

NO

Please

Per piacere / Per favore

PER PEE-ah-CHE'-RE
PER Fah-VO'-RE

Always remember to say **please** and **thank you**.

Thank you

Grazie

GRah'-TSEE-e

Excuse me

Mi scusi

MEE SKoo'-ZEE

I'm sorry

Mi dispiace

MEE DEES-PEE-ah'-CHE

I'm a tourist.

Sono un turista. (m)

SŌ-NŌ ⓄN TOO-RĒS-Tah

I'm a tourist.

Sono una turista. (f)

SŌ-NŌ OO-Nah TOO-RĒS-Tah

I do not speak Italian.

Non parlo italiano.

NŌN Pah́R-LŌ ĒE-Tah-LĒE-ah́-NŌ

I speak a little Italian.

Parlo un poco italiano.

Pah́R-LŌ ⓄN PŌ-KŌ
ĒE-Tah-LĒE-ah́-NŌ

Do you understand English?

Capisce l'inglese?

Kah-PĒE-SHē LĒEN-GLē-Sē

I don't understand!

Non capisco!

NŌN Kah-PĒES-KŌ

Please repeat.

Ripeta, per favore.

RĒE-Pē-Tah PēR Fah-VŌ-Rē

FEELINGS

I want…

Voglio...

VOⒺL-YO…

I have…

Ho…

Ⓞ…

I know.

Lo so.

LO SO

I don't know.

Non lo so.

NON LO SO

I like it.

Mi piace.

MⒺ PⒺ-ⓐ-CHⓔ

I don't like it.

Non mi piace.

NON MⒺ PⒺ-ⓐ-CHⓔ

I'm lost.

Mi sono perduto. (male) Mi sono perduta. (female)

MEE SO-NO PER-DOO-TO (ah)

I'm in a hurry.

Ho fretta.

O FRET-Tah

I'm tired.

Sono stanco. (male) Sono stanca. (female)

SO-NO STah-N-KO (ah)

I'm ill.

Sono ammalato. (male) Sono ammalata. (female)

SO-NO ahM-Mah-Lah-TO (ah)

I'm hungry.

Ho fame.

O Fah-ME

I'm thirsty.

Ho sete.

O SE-TE

I'm angry.

Sono arrabbiato. (male) Sono arrabbiata. (female)

SO-NO ah-Rah-B-BEE-ah-TO (ah)

EPLS displays the feminine ending in parenthesis.

INTRODUCTIONS

My name is…

Mi chiamo…

MEE KEE-ah-MO…

What's your name?

Come si chiama?

KO-ME SEE KEE-ah-Mah

Where are you from?

Di dov'è Lei?

DEE DO-VE LE-EE

Do you live here?

Lei abita qui?

LE-EE ah-BEE-Tah KWEE

I just arrived.

Sono appena arrivato.

SO-NO ah-P-PE-Nah ah-REE-Vah-TO

What hotel are you [staying] at?

In quale hotel sta?

EEN KWah-LE O-TEL STah

I'm at the…hotel.

Sono all' hotel...

SŌ-NO ⓐL Ⓞ-TⓔL...

It was nice to meet you.

È stato un piacere incontrarla.

Ⓔ STⓐ-TO ⓄN PⒺ-ⓐ-CHⓔ-Rⓔ
ⒺN-KON-TRⓐR-Lⓐ

See you tomorrow.

Ci vediamo domani.

CHⒺ Vⓔ-DⒺ-ⓐ-MO DŌ-Mⓐ-NⒺ

See you next time.

Arrivederci a presto.

ⓐ-RⒺ-Vⓔ-DⓔR-CHⒺ ⓐ PRⓔS-TO

See you later.

A più tardi.

ⓐ PⒺ-Ⓞ Tⓐ R-DⒺ

Good luck!

Buona fortuna!

BWŌ-Nⓐ FⓄR-TⓄ-Nⓐ

THE BIG QUESTIONS

Who?

Chi?

KĒ

Who is it?

Chi è?

KĒ ě

What?

Cosa?

KŌ-Zah

What's that?

Che cos'è quello?

Kě KŌŌ-Zě KWěL-LŌ

When?

Quando?

KWahN-DŌ

Where?

Dove?

DŌ-Vě

Where is…?

Dov'è...?

DO-Vê...

Which?

Quale?

KWah-Lê

Why?

Perchè?

PêR-Kê

How?

Come?

KO-Mê

How much? (does it cost)

Quanto costa?

KWahN-TO KOS-Tah

How long?

Per quanto tempo?

PêR KWahN-TO TêM-PO

ASKING FOR THINGS

The following phrases are valuable for directions, food, help, etc.

I would like...

Vorrei....

VO-RĕE´-EE...

I need...

Ho bisogno di...

O BEE-ZON-YO DEE...

Can you...

Può...?

PWO...

When asking for things be sure to say <u>please</u> and <u>thank you</u>.

Please	**Thank you**
Per piacere	Grazie
PĕR PEE-ah-CHĕ´-Rĕ	GRah´-TSEE-ĕ

PHRASEMAKER

Combine **I would like** with the
following phrases beneath, and
you will have a good idea how to ask for things.

I would like...

Vorrei... per piacere

V⓪-Ɍⓔ-ⒺⒺ... PPC

▸ **more coffee**

ancora del caffè

ⓐⓗN-Ⓚⓞ-Ɍⓐⓗ Dⓔ L Ⓚⓐⓗ-Fⓔ

▸ **some water**

dell'acqua

Dⓔ L Lⓐⓗ-ⓀWⓐⓗ

▸ **some ice**

del ghiaccio

Dⓔ L GⒺⒺ-ⓐⓗ-CHⓞ

▸ **the menu**

il menù

ⒺⒺL Mⓔ-N⚭

PHRASEMAKER

Here are a few sentences you can use when you feel the urge to say **I need...** or **Can you...**?

I need...
Ho bisogno...

Ⓞ Bⓔⓔ-ZOⓝ-Yⓞ....

▸ **help**
d'aiuto

Dⓐⓗ-Yⓞⓞ-Tⓞ

▸ **directions**
di indicazioni

Dⓔⓔ ⓔⓔN-Dⓔⓔ-Kⓐⓗ-TSⓔⓔ-Ⓞ-Nⓔⓔ

▸ **more money**
di più soldi

Dⓔⓔ Pⓔⓔ-ⓞⓞ SOⓛ-Dⓔⓔ

▸ **change**
di moneta

Dⓔⓔ MOⓝ-Nⓔ-Tⓐⓗ

▸ **a lawyer**
di un avvocato

Dⓔⓔ ⓞⓞN ⓐⓗV-VOⓝ-Kⓐⓗ-Tⓞ

PHRASEMAKER

Can you...

Può...

PW◎...

▶ **help me?**

aiutarmi?

@h-Y◎◎-T@hR-M㏄

▶ **show me?**

indicarmi?

㏇N-D㏄-K@hR-M㏄

▶ **give me...?**

darmi...?

D@hR-M㏄

▶ **tell me...?**

dirmi...?

D㏄R-M㏄

▶ **take me to...?**

portarmi al...?

P◎R-T@hR-M㏄ @hL...

ASKING THE WAY

No matter how independent you are, sooner or later you'll probably have to ask for directions.

Where is...?

Dov'è...?

DⓄ-VⒺ̀...

Is it near?

È vicino?

Ⓔ̀ VⒺⒺ-CHⒺⒺ́-NⓄ

Is it far?

È lontano?

Ⓔ̀ LⓄN-Tⓐⓗ́-NⓄ

I'm looking for...

Sto cercando...

STⓄ CHⒺ̃R-KⓐⓗN-DⓄ...

I'm lost! (male)

Mi sono perduto!

MⒺⒺ SⓄ́-NⓄ PⒺ̃R-DⓄⓄ́-TⓄ

I'm lost! (female)

Mi sono perduta!

MⒺⒺ SⓄ́-NⓄ PⒺ̃R-DⓄⓄ́-Tⓐⓗ

PHRASEMAKER

Where is...

Dov'è...

D(o)-V(ĕ)...

▸ **the restroom?**

la toilette?

L(ah) TW(ah)-L(ĕ)T

▸ **the telephone?**

il telefono?

(ee)L T(ĕ)-L(ĕ)-F(o)-N(o)

▸ **the beach?**

la spiaggia?

L(ah) SP(ee)-(ah)-J(ah)

▸ **the hotel...?**

l'hotel...?

L(o)-T(ĕ)L

▸ **the train for...?**

il treno per...?

(ee)L TR(ĕ)-N(o) P(ĕ)R...

TIME

What time is it?

Che ora è?

K~e~ O´-R~ah~ ~e~

Morning

Mattino

M~ah~T-T~EE~´-N~O~

Noon

Mezzogiorno

M~e~-TS~O~-J~O~´R-N~O~

Night

Notte

N~O~´T-T~e~

Today

Oggi

~O~´-J~EE~

Tomorrow

Domani

D~O~-M~ah~´-N~EE~

This week

Questa settimana

KWĕS-Tah SĕT-TEE-Mah-Nah

This month

Questo mese

KWĕS-TO Mĕ-Sĕ

This year

Quest'anno

KWĕST-ahN-NO

Now

Adesso

ah-DĕS-SO

Soon

Presto

PRĕS-TO

Later

Più tardi

PEE-oo TahR-DEE

Never

Mai

Mah-EE

WHO IS IT?

I

Io

You (Formal)	**You** (Informal)
Lei	Tu
L Ĕ-ĒĒ	T ᴏᴏ
Use this form of **you** with people you don't know well.	Use this form of **you** with people you know well.

He

Lui

L ᴏᴏ-ĒĒ

She

Lei

L Ĕ-ĒĒ

We

Noi

N ᴏʏ

They

Loro

L Ō-Ŗō

THE, A (AN), AND SOME

To use the correct form of **The**, **A (An)**, or **Some**, you must know if the Italian word is masculine or feminine. Often you will have to guess! If you make a mistake, you will still be understood.

The

Il, Lo, L'

ⒺⒺL / LⓄ / L

The before a singular masculine noun:
(il) boy is handsome.

I, Gli

ⒺⒺ / LYⒺⒺ

The before a plural masculine noun:
(i) boys are handsome.

La

LⓐⒽ

The before a singular feminine noun:
(la) woman is pretty.

I, Le

ⒺⒺ / LⒺ

The before a plural feminine noun:
(i) women are pretty.

A, An

Un / Uno

ⓄⓄN / ⓄⓄ-NⓄ

A or **an** before a masculine noun:
He is (un) man.

Una / Un'

ⓄⓄN-ⓐⒽ / ⓄⓄN

A or **an** before a feminine noun:
She is (una) woman.

Some

Qualche

KWⓐⒽL-KⒺ

Some before masculine and feminine nouns.

USEFUL OPPOSITES

Near	**Far**
Vicino	Lontano
VEE-CHEE-NO	LON-Tah-NO

Here	**There**
Qui	Là
KWEE	Lah

Left (direction)	**Right** (direction)
Sinistra	Destra
SEE-NEE'S-TRah	De͞S-TRah

A little	**A lot**
Un poco	Molto
OON PO'-KO	MOL-TO

More	**Less**
Di più	Meno
DEE PEE-OO'	Me͞-NO

Big	**Small**
Grande	Piccolo
GRah'N-De͞	PEE'K-KO-LO

Open	**Closed**
Aperto	Chiuso
ah-PĚR-TO	KYOO-ZO
Cheap	**Expensive**
A buon mercato	Caro
ah BWON MĔR-Kah-TO	Kah-RO
Clean	**Dirty**
Pulito	Sporco
POO-LĒE-TO	SPŎR-KO
Good	**Bad**
Buono	Cattivo
BWŌ-NO	Kah-T-TĒE-VO
Vacant	**Occupied**
Libero	Occupato
LĒE-BĕR-RO	O-KOO-Pah-TO
Right	**Wrong**
Giusto	Sbagliato
JOOS-TO	SBah-L-Yah-TO

WORDS OF ENDEARMENT

I love you.

Ti amo.

T\overline{EE} \overline{ah}'-M\overline{O}

My love

Amore mio

\overline{ah}-M\overline{O}'-R\breve{e} M\overline{EE}'-\overline{O}

My life

Vita mia

V\overline{EE}'-T\overline{ah} M\overline{EE}'-\overline{ah}

My friend (to a male)

Amico mio

\overline{ah}-M\overline{EE}'-K\overline{O} M\overline{EE}'-\overline{O}

My friend (to a female)

Amica mia

\overline{ah}-M\overline{EE}'-K\overline{ah} M\overline{EE}'-\overline{ah}

Kiss me!

Baciami!

B\overline{ah}'-CH\overline{ah}-M\overline{EE}

WORDS OF ANGER !!!

What do you want?

Che cosa vuole?

Kĕ KŌ-Zah VWŌ-Lĕ

Leave me alone!

Mi lasci in pace!

MEE Lah-SHEE EEN Pah-CHĕ

Go away!

Vada via!

Vah-Dah VEE-ah

Stop bothering me!

Non mi stia a seccare!

NON MEE STEE-ah ah Sĕk-Kah-Rĕ

Be quiet!

Silenzio!

SEE-LĕN-TSEE-O

That's enough!

Basta!

Bah-S-Tah

COMMON EXPRESSIONS

When you are at a loss for words but have the feeling you should say something, try one of these!

Who knows?

Chi lo sa?

K(EE) L(O) S(ah)

That's the truth!

E' la verità!

(ē) L(ah) V(ē)-R(EE)-T(ah)

Sure!

Sicuro!

S(EE)-K(oo)-R(O)

Wow!

Che sorpresa!

K(ē) S(O)R-PR(ē)-Z(ah)

What's happening?

Che cosa succede?

K(ē) K(O)-Z(ah) S(oo)-CH(ē)-D(ē)

I think so.

Penso di sí.

P(ē)N-S(O) D(EE) S(EE)

Cheers!

Salute!

Sah-LOO-Tĕ

Good luck!

Buona fortuna!

BWŌ-Nah FOB-TOO-Nah

With pleasure!

Con piacere!

KON PEE-ah-CHĕ-Rĕ

My goodness!

Per l'amor del cielo!

PĕB Lah-MŌB DĕL CHĕ-LO

What a shame! / That's too bad!

Peccato!

PĕK-Kah-TO

Well done! Bravo!

Bene! / Bravo!

Bĕ-Nĕ / BBah-VO

USEFUL COMMANDS

Stop!

Alt!

@LT

Go!

Forza!

FOR-TS@

Wait!

Aspetti!

@-SPET-TEE

Hurry!

Abbia fretta!

@B-BEE-Y@ FRET-T@

Slow down!

Rallenti!

R@L-LEN-TEE

Come here!

Venga qui!

VEN-G@ KWEE

Help!

Aiuto!

@-YOO-TO

EMERGENCIES

Fire!

Al fuoco!

ⓐL FWOʹ-KO

Emergency!

Emergenza!

ⓔ-MⓔB-JⓔʹN-TSⓐ

Call the police!

Chiamate la polizia!

Kⓔⓔ-ⓐ-Mⓐʹ-Tⓔ Lⓐ PO-Lⓔⓔ-TSⓔⓔʹ-ⓐ

Call a doctor!

Chiamate un medico!

Kⓔⓔ-ⓐ-Mⓐʹ-Tⓔ ⓞⓞN Mⓔʹ-Dⓔⓔ-KO

Call an ambulance!

Chiamate un' ambulanza!

Kⓔⓔ-ⓐ-Mⓐʹ-Tⓔ ⓞⓞN
ⓐM-Bⓞⓞ-LⓐʹN-TSⓐ

I need help!

Ho bisogno d'aiuto!

O Bⓔⓔ-ZOʹN-YO Dⓐ-Yⓞⓞʹ-TO

ARRIVAL

Passing through customs should be easy since there are usually agents available who speak English. You may be asked how long you intend to stay and if you have anything to declare.

- Have your passport ready.

- Be sure all documents are up-to-date.

- While in a foreign country, it is wise to keep receipts for everything you buy.

- Be aware that many countries will charge a departure tax when you leave. Your travel agent should be able to find out if this affects you.

- If you have connecting flights, be sure to reconfirm them in advance.

- Make sure your luggage is clearly marked inside and out.

- Take valuables and medicines in carry-on bags.

SIGNS TO LOOK FOR:

DOGANA (Customs)

BAGAGLI (Baggage)

KEY WORDS

Baggage

Bagaglio

B@-G@L-YO

Customs

Dogana

DO-G@-N@

Documents

Documenti

DO-KOO-MĚN-TEE

Passport

Passaporto

P@S-S@-POR-TO

Porter

Facchino

F@-KEE-NO

Tax

Imposta

EEM-POS-T@

USEFUL PHRASES

Here is my passport.

Ecco il mio passaporto.

É-KO EL MÉE-O
PahS-Sah-PÓR-TO

I have nothing to declare.

Non ho nulla da dichiarare.

NON O NOOL-Lah Dah
DEE-KEE-ah-Rah-RÉ

I'm here on business.

Sono in viaggio d'affari.

SÓ-NO EN VEE-ah-JO
DahF-Fah-REE

I'm here on vacation.

Sono in vacanza.

SÓ-NO EN Vah-KahN-TSah

Is there a problem?

C'è un problema?

CHÉ OON PRO-BLÉ-Mah

PHRASEMAKER

I'll be staying…

Resterò qui…

RĔS-TĔ́-RŌ KWĒĒ…

▸ **one week**

una settimana

ŌṒ-Nah SĔT-TĒĒ-Mah́-Nah

▸ **two weeks**

due settimane

DŌṒ-ĕ SĔT-TĒĒ-Mah́-Nĕ

▸ **one month**

un mese

ŌŌN MĔ́-Zĕ

▸ **two months**

due mesi

DŌṒ-ĕ MĔ́-ZĒĒ

USEFUL PHRASES

I need a porter!

Ho bisogno di un facchino!

Ⓞ BⒺⒺ-ZⓄⓄN-YⓄ DⒺⒺ
ⓄⓄN Fⓐ-KⒺⒺ-NⓄ

These are my bags.

Queste sono le mie valigie.

KWⒺS-TⒺ SⓄ-NⓄ LⒺ
MⒺⒺ-Ⓔ Vⓐ-LⒺⒺ-Jⓐ

I'm missing a bag.

Mi manca una valigie.

MⒺⒺ Mⓐ N-Kⓐ ⓄⓄ-Nⓐ Vⓐ-LⒺⒺ-Jⓐ

Take my bags to a taxi, please.

Per favore, porti le mie valigie al tassì.

PⒺR Fⓐ-VⓄ-RⒺ
PⓄR-TⒺ LⒺ MⒺⒺ-Ⓔ
Vⓐ-LⒺⒺ-JⒺ ⓐL Tⓐ K-SⒺⒺ

Thank you. This is for you.

Grazie. Questo è per lei.

GRⓐ-TSⒺⒺ-Ⓔ.
KWⒺS-TⓄ Ⓔ PⒺR LⒺ-ⒺⒺ

PHRASEMAKER

Where is…

Dov'è…

DⓄ-Vⓔ́…

▸ **customs?**

la dogana?

Lⓐ DⓄ-Gⓐ́-Nⓐ

▸ **baggage claim?**

il ritiro bagagli?

ⒺL RⒺⒺ-TⒺⒺ́-RⓄ Bⓐ-Gⓐ́L-YⒺⒺ

▸ **the money exchange?**

l'ufficio di cambio?

LⓄⓄ-FⒺⒺ́-CHⓄ DⒺⒺ Kⓐ́M-BⒺⒺ-Ⓞ

▸ **the taxi stand?**

il posteggio di tassì?

ⒺL PⓄ-STⒺ́-JⓄ DⒺⒺ Tⓐ́K-SⒺⒺ

▸ **the bus stop?**

la fermata dell'autobus?

Lⓐ FⒺ́R-Mⓐ-Tⓐ DⒺL ⓄⓌ-TⓄ-BⓄⓄS

HOTEL SURVIVAL

A wide selection of accommodations, ranging from the most basic to the most extravagant, are available wherever you travel in Italy. When booking your room, find out what amenities are included for the price you pay.

- Make reservations well in advance and get written confirmation of your reservations before you leave home.

- Always have identification ready when checking in.

- Do not leave valuables, prescriptions, or cash in your room when you are not there!

- Electrical items like blow-dryers may need an adapter. Your hotel may be able to provide one, but to be safe, take one with you.

- Although a service charge is usually included on your bill, it is customary to tip maids, bellhops, and doormen.

KEY WORDS

Hotel

Hotel

Ⓞ-TⒺ́L

Bellman

Fattorino

FⓐT-TⓄ-RⒺ́E-NⓄ

Maid

Cameriera

Kⓐ-MⒺ-RⒺE-Ⓔ́-Rⓐ

Message

Messaggio

MⒺS-Sⓐ́-JⓄ

Reservation

Prenotazione

PRⒺ-NⓄ-Tⓐ-TSⒺE-Ó-NⒺ

Room service

Servizio in camera

SⒺR-VⒺE-TSⒺE-Ⓞ ⒺN Kⓐ́-MⒺ-Rⓐ

CHECKING IN

My name is...

Mi chiamo...

Mê Kê-ah-M⊙...

I have a reservation.

Ho una prenotazione.

⊙ ⊙⊙-Nah PRê-N⊙-Tah-TSê-⊙-Nê

Have you any vacancies?

Avete stanze libere?

ah-Vê-Tê STah-N-TSê Lêê-Bê-Rê

What is the charge per night?

Quanto costa per notte?

KWah-N-T⊙ K⊙S-Tah PêR N⊙T-Tê

Is there room service?

C'è il servizio in camera?

CHê êL SêR-Vêê-TSê-⊙ êN
Kah-Mê-Rah

PHRASEMAKER

I would like a room with…

Vorrei una stanza con…

VO-R̆ē-EE ōō-Nah STaĥN-TSah KON…

▶ **a bath**

un bagno

ōōN Bah́N-YO

▶ **one bed**

un letto

ōōN LĕT-TO

▶ **two beds**

due letti

Dōō-ĕ LĕT-TEE

▶ **a shower**

una doccia

ōō-Nah DO-CHah

▶ **a view**

vista

VEE-S-Tah

USEFUL PHRASES

Where is the dining room?

Dov'è la sala da pranzo?

D⊙⊙-Vě́ Lah Sah́-Lah Dah PRah́N-TS⊙

Are meals included?

I pasti sono inclusi?

EE Pah́S-TEE S⊙́-N⊙ EEN-KL⊙⊙́-ZEE

What time is breakfast?

A che ora è la colazione?

ah Kě ⊙́-Rah ě Lah
K⊙-Lah́-TSEE-⊙́-Ně

What time is lunch?

A che ora è il pranzo?

ah Kě ⊙́-Rah ě EEL PRah́N-TS⊙

What time is dinner?

A che ora è la cena?

ah Kě ⊙́-Rah ě Lah CHě́-Nah

My room key, please.

La chiave, per favore.

L⒜ K⒠⒠-⒜́-V⒠ P⒠R F⒜-VO̅́-R⒠

Are there any messages for me?

Ci sono dei messaggi per me?

CH⒠⒠ SO̅́-NO̅ D⒠⒠⒠ M⒠S-S⒜́-J⒠⒠
P⒠R M⒠

Please wake me at...

Per favore mi svegli alle...

P⒠R F⒜-VO̅́-R⒠ M⒠⒠Z
V⒠́L-Y⒠⒠ ⒜́L-L⒠...

6:00	6:30
sei	sei e mezzo
S⒠́-⒠⒠	S⒠́-⒠⒠ ⒠ M⒠́-TS○

7:00	7:30
sette	sette e mezzo
S⒠́T-T⒠	S⒠́T-T⒠ ⒠ M⒠́-TS○

8:00	8:30
otto	otto e mezzo
○́T-T○	○́T-T○ ⒠ M⒠́-TS○

9:00	9:30
nove	nove e mezzo
NO̅́-V⒠	NO̅́-V⒠ ⒠ M⒠́-TS○

PHRASEMAKER

I need…

Ho bisogno...

Ⓞ BⒺⒺ-ZⓄN-YⓄ...

▸ **a babysitter**

di una babysitter

DⒺⒺ ⓄⓄ′-Nⓐⓗ BⒺ-BⒺⒺ-SⒺⒺ′-TⒺⓇ

▸ **a bellman**

di un fattorino

DⒺⒺ ⓄⓄN FⓐⓗT-TⓄ-RⒺⒺ′-NⓄ

▸ **more blankets**

di altre coperte

DⒺⒺ ⓐⓗL-TRⒺ KⓄ-PⒺⓇ-TⒺ

▸ **a hotel safe**

di una cassaforte

DⒺⒺ ⓄⓄ′-Nⓐⓗ Kⓐⓗ-Sⓐⓗ-FⓄⓇ-TⒺ

▸ **ice cubes**

di cubetti di ghiaccio

DⒺⒺ KⓄⓄ-BⒺⒺ′T-TⒺⒺ DⒺⒺ GⒺⒺ-ⓐⓗ′-CHⓄ

▶ **an extra key**

di una chiave extra

DEE OO-Nah KEE-ah-VEe EeKS-TRah

▶ **a maid**

di una cameriera

DEE OO-Nah Kah-MEe-REE-Ee-Bah

▶ **the manager**

del direttore

DEeL DEE-REeT-TO-REe

▶ **clean sheets**

di lenzuola pulite

DEE LEeN-TSWO-Lah POO-LEE-TEE

▶ **soap**

di sapone

DEE Sah-PO-NEe

▶ **toilet paper**

di carta igienica

DEE Kah-B-Tah EE-JEe-NEE-Kah

▶ **more towels**

di altri asciugamani

DEE ahL-TREE ah-SHOO-Gah-Mah-NEE

PHRASEMAKER
(PROBLEMS)

There is no...

Manca...

M@h'N-K@h...

▸ **electricity**

la corrente

L@h   K⓪-R€'N-T€

▸ **heat**

il riscaldamento

€L   R€ES-K@h-L-D@h-M€'N-T⓪

▸ **hot water**

l'acqua calda

L@h'-KW@h   K@hL-D@h

▸ **light**

la luce

L@h   L⓪⓪'-CH€

▸ **toilet paper**

la carta igienica

L@h   K@h'R-T@h   €E-J€'-N€E-K@h

PHRASEMAKER
(SPECIAL NEEDS)

Do you have…

Avete...

ⓐ-Vⓔ́-Tⓔ...

▸ **an elevator?**

un ascensore?

ⓄⓄN ⓐ-SHⓔN-SÓ-Bⓔ

▸ **a ramp?**

una rampa d'accesso?

ⓄⓄ́-Nⓐ Bⓐ́M-Pⓐ Dⓐ-CHⓔ́-SⓄ

▸ **a wheelchair?**

una sedia a rotelle?

ⓄⓄ́-Nⓐ Sⓔ́D-Yⓐ ⓐ BⓄ-Tⓔ́L-Lⓔ

▸ **facilities for the disabled?**

accomodamenti per gli handicappati?

ⓐ-KⓄ-MⓄ-Dⓐ-Mⓔ́N-TEE Pⓔ̃B GLEE
ⓐN-DEE-Kⓐ́P-Pⓐ́-TEE

CHECKING OUT

I would like the bill, please.

Vorrei il conto, per favore.

VO-Rё-EE EL KON-TO PF

Is this bill correct?

Questo conto è esatto?

KWёS-TO KON-TO ё ё-ZahT-TO

Do you accept credit cards?

Accettate carte di credito?

ah-CHё-Tah-Tё KahR-Tё DEE
KRё-DEE-TO

Could you have my luggage brought down?

Potrebbe far portare giù le mie valigie?

PO-TRёB-B-Bё FahR POR-Tah-Rё
Joo Lё MEE-ё VahL-EE-Jё

Can you call a taxi for me?

Potrebbe chiamarmi un tassi?

PO-TRĕB-Bĕ KEE-ah-MahR-MEE
ooN TãK-SEE

I had a very good time!

Ho passato dei giorni bellissimi!

O PahS-Sah-TO Dĕ JOR-NEE
BĕL-LEES-SEE-MEE

Thanks for everything.

Grazie di tutto.

GRah-TSEE Dĕ TooT-TO

I'll see you next time.

Arrivederci a presto.

ah-REE-Vĕ-DĕR-CHEE ah PRĕS-TO

Good-bye

Arrivederci

ah-REE-Vĕ-DĕR-CHEE

RESTAURANT SURVIVAL

Italy is famous for its cuisine. You are encouraged to enjoy the wide variety of regional specialties. Don't forget to try the many excellent Italian white wines and robust red wines!

- Breakfast, **la prima colazione**, is usually served at your hotel. Lunch, **il pranzo**, normally served from noon to 3 PM, and dinner, **la cena**, from 7 PM to 10 PM.

- Taste Italian cooking at the best-known **restaurantes** in the cities or try the many small **trattories** available. Many mouth-watering dishes await the adventurous traveler.

- **Pane e Coperto** indicates bread and cover charge. Most restaurants will have a cover charge and you will be charged even if you don't eat the bread!

- Some restaurants have a stand-up bar where you can order food and drinks with no cover charge.

- A **ristorante** offers fine dining and usually opens around 8:00 PM.

KEY WORDS

Breakfast

Colazione

KO-Lah-TSEE-O-Ne

Lunch

Pranzo

PRah'N-TSO

Dinner

Cena

CHe'-Nah

Waiter

Cameriere

Kah-Me-REE-e-Re

Waitress

Cameriera

Kah-Me-REE-e-Rah

Restaurant

Ristorante

REES-TO-Rah'N-Te

USEFUL PHRASES

A table for…

Un tavolo per...

ⓄN Tⓐⓗ-VⓄ-LⓄ PⓔⓇ…

2	4	6
due	quattro	sei
Dⓞⓞ-ⓔ	KWⓐⓗT-TⓇⓄ	SⒶ

The menu, please.

Il menù, per favore.

ⒺL Mⓔ-Nⓞⓞ PF

Separate checks, please.

Conti separati, per favore.

KⓞⓞN-Tⓔⓔ Sⓔ-Pⓐⓗ-Ⓡⓐⓗ-Tⓔⓔ PF

We are in a hurry.

Abbiamo fretta.

ⓐB-Bⓔⓔ-ⓐⓗ-MⓄ FⓇⓔT-Tⓐⓗ

What do you recommend?

Che cosa consiglia?

Kⓔ KⓄ-Zⓐⓗ KⓄN-SⓔⓔL-Yⓐⓗ

Please bring me…

Per favore, mi porti...

PĕR Fah-VO'-Rĕ Mēē PO'R-Tēē

Please bring us…

Per favore ci porti...

PĕR Fah-VO'-Rĕ CHēē PO'R-Tēē

I'm hungry.

Ho fame.

O Fah'-Mĕ

I'm thirsty.

Ho sete.

O Sĕ'-Tĕ

Is service included?

Il servizio é incluso?

ēēL Sĕr-Vēē'-TSēē-O ĕ ēēN-KLoo'-ZO

I would like the bill, please.

Vorrei il conto, per favore.

VO-Rĕ'-ēē ēēL
KO'N-TO PF

PHRASEMAKER

Ordering beverages is easy and a great way to practice your Italian! In many foreign countries you will have to request ice with your drinks.

Please bring me...

Per favore, mi porti...

PⒺR Fⓐh-VO-RⒺ MEE POR-TEE...

▶ **coffee**

del caffè

DⒺL Kⓐh-FⒺ

▶ **tea**

del tè

DⒺL TⒺ

▶ **with cream**

con panna

KON Pⓐh'N-Nⓐh

▶ **with sugar**

con zucchero

KON TSⓞⓞ'-KⒺ-RO

▶ **with lemon**

con limone

KON LEE-MO-NⒺ

▶ **with ice**

con ghiaccio

KON GEE-ⓐh'-CHO

Soft drinks

Bibite

BEE-BEE-Tẽ

Milk

Latte

LahT-Tẽ

Hot chocolate

Cioccolata calda

CHOK-KO-Lah-Tah KahL-Duh

Juice

Succo

TSOOK-KO

Orange juice

Succo d'arancia

TSOO-KO DEE ah-RahN-CHah

Ice water

Acqua con ghiaccio

ah-KWah KON GEE-ah-CHO

Mineral water

Acqua minerale

ah-KWah MEE-Nẽ-Rah-Lẽ

AT THE BAR

Bartender

Barista

B@h-R@ES-T@h

The wine list, please.

La lista dei vini, per favore.

L@h LEES-T@h DEE VEE-NEE PF

Cocktail

Cocktail

K@K-T@L

On the rocks

Con ghiaccio

K@N GEE-@h-CH@

Straight

Senza ghiaccio

S@N-TS@h GEE-@h-CH@

With lemon

Con limone

K@N L@E-M@-N@

PHRASEMAKER

I would like a glass of…

Vorrei un bicchiere di...

VO-RĕE-EE OON BEEK-Yĕ-Rĕ DEE…

▸ **champagne**

champagne

SHahM-PahN-Yah

▸ **beer**

birra

BEER-Rah

▸ **wine**

vino

VEE-NO

▸ **red wine**

vino rosso

VEE-NO ROS-SO

▸ **white wine**

vino bianco

VEE-NO BEE-ahN-KO

Complement your meal with a variety of choices of sparkling wines, chiantis, liqueurs, and the grappas!

ORDERING BREAKFAST

In Italy, breakfast is usually small, consisting of a croissant or warm bread with butter and jam accompanied by café au lait, hot tea, or hot chocolate.

Bread

Pane

Pah-Neh

Toast

Pane tostato

Pah-Neh TOS-Tah-TO

---

with butter

con burro

KON Boo-BO

---

with jam

con marmellata

KON Mah-B-Meh-L-Lah-Dah

Cereal

Cereali

CHeh-Beh-ah-Lee

PHRASEMAKER

I would like…

Vorrei...

VO'-Ⓡⓔ-ⒺⒺ...

▶ **two eggs…**

due uova...

Dⓞⓞ'-ⓔ WO'-Vⓐⓗ

▶ **scrambled**

strapazzate

STRⓐⓗ-Pⓐⓗ-TSⓐⓗ-Tⓔ

▶ **fried**

fritte

FRⒺⒺT-Tⓔ

▶ **with bacon**

con pancetta

KON PⓐⓗN-CHⓔ'-Tⓐⓗ

▶ **with ham**

con prosciutto

KON PRO-SHⓞⓞT-TO

▶ **with potatoes**

con patate

KON Pⓐⓗ-Tⓐⓗ'-Tⓔ

LUNCH AND DINNER

Although you are encouraged to sample great Italian cuisine, it is important to be able to order foods you are familiar with. This section will provide words and phrases to help you.

I would like…

Vorrei....

VO-R̃ē-EE…

We would like…

Vorremmo...

VO-R̃ēM-MO…

Please bring us…

Per favore ci porti...

PēR Fah-VO-R̃ē CHEE POR-TEE…

The lady would like…

La signora vorrebbe...

Lah SEEN-YO-R̃ah VO-R̃ēB-Bē…

The gentleman would like…

Il signore vorrebbe...

EEL SEEN-YO-R̃ē VO-R̃ēB-Bē…

STARTERS

Appetizers
Antipasti

@N-T⒠-P@S-T⒠

Bread and butter
Pane e burro

P@-N⒠ ⒠ B⒪-R⓪

Cheese
Formaggio

F⓪R-M@-J⓪

Fruit
Frutta

FR⒪T-T@

Salad
Insalata

⒠N-S@-L@-T@

Soup
Zuppa

TS⒪P-P@

MEATS

Bacon
Pancetta
P@N-CH@T-T@

Beef
Manzo
M@N-TS©

Beef steak
Bistecca
B©S-T@K-K@

Ham
Prosciutto
PR©-SH©©T-T©

Lamb
Agnello
@N-Y©L-L©

Pork
Maiale
M@-Y@-L©

Veal
Vitello
V©-T©L-L©

POULTRY

Roasted chicken

Pollo al forno

PÓL-LO ⓐL FÓR-NO

Broiled chicken

Pollo alla griglia

PÓL-LO ⓐL-Lⓐ GRⒺⒺ-Yⓐ

Fried chicken

Pollo fritto

PÓL-LO FRⒺⒺT-TO

Duck

Anatra

ⓐ-Nⓐ-TRⓐ

Goose

Oca

Ó-Kⓐ

Turkey

Tacchino

Tⓐ-KⒺⒺ-NO

SEAFOOD

Fish
Pesce
PÉ-SHÉ

Lobster
Aragosta
ah-Rah-GŌS-Tah

Oysters
Ostriche
ŌS-TREE-KÉ

Salmon
Salmone
Sah-L-MŌ-NÉ

Shrimp
Gamberetti
Gah-M-BÉ-RÉT-TEE

Trout
Trota
TRŌ-Tah

Tuna
Tonno
TŌN-NŌ

OTHER ENTREES

Sandwich
Panino
P@h-N@E-N@

Hot dog
Hot dog
@hT D@hG

Hamburger
Hamburger
@hM-B@@-G@R

French fries
Patatine fritte
P@h-T@h-T@E-N@ FR@ET-T@

Pasta
Pasta
P@hS-T@h

Pizza
Pizza
P@ET-S@h

VEGETABLES

Carrots

Carote

Kah-RO-Te

Corn

Granturco

GRahN-TooR-KO

Mushrooms

Funghi

FooN-GEE

Onions

Cipolle

CHEE-POL-Le

Potatoes

Patate

Pah-Tah-Te

Rice

Riso

REE-ZO

Tomato

Pomodoro

PO-MO-DO-RO

FRUITS

Apple

Mela

Mĕ́-Lah

Banana

Banana

Bah-Nah́-Nah

Grapes

Uva

oó-Vah

Lemon

Limone

Lēē-Mó-Nĕ

Orange

Arancia

ah-Bah́N-CHah

Strawberry

Fragola

FRah́-GO-Lah

Watermelon

Anguria

ahN-Goó-Bēē-ah

DESSERTS

Desserts

Dolci

DŌL-CHEE

Apple pie

Crostata di mela

KROS-Tah-Tah DEE MĔ-Lah

Cherry pie

Crostata di ciliegia

KROS-Tah-Tah DEE CHEEL-YĔ-Jah

Pastries

Pasticcini

PahS-TEE-CHEE-NEE

Candy

Caramella

Kah-Rah-MĔL-Lah

Order a refreshing strawberry or lemon sorbet as the perfect
end to your lovely Italian meal!

Ice cream

Gelato

JĕL-Lah́-TO

Ice-cream cone

Cono di gelato

KO-́NO DEE JĕL-Lah́-TO

Chocolate

Cioccolato

CHOK-KO-Lah́-TO

Strawberry

Fragola

FRah́-GO-Lah

Vanilla

Vaniglia

Vah-NEEL-Yah

CONDIMENTS

Butter
Burro
B͞oo-R͞O

Ketchup
Ketchup
Kĕ-CH͞oo͞P

Mayonnaise
Maionese
Mah-Y͞O-Nĕ-Sĕ

Mustard
Senape
Sĕ-Nah-Pĕ

Salt   **Pepper**
Sale   Pepe
Sah-Lĕ   Pĕ-Pĕ

Sugar
Zucchero
TS͞oo-Kĕ-R͞O

Vinegar and oil
Aceto e olio
ah-CHĕ-T͞O   ĕ   ͞OL-Y͞O

SETTINGS

A cup
Una tazza
 OO-Nah Tah-TSah

A glass
Un bicchiere
OON BEEK-Yё-Rё

A spoon
Un cucchiaio
OON KOOK-Yah-YO

A fork
Una forchetta
OO-Nah FOR-KёT-Tah

A knife
Un coltello
OON KOL-TёL-LO

A plate
Un piatto
OON PEE-ah T-TO

A napkin
Un tovagliolo
OON TO-Vah L-YO-LO

HOW DO YOU WANT IT COOKED?

Baked

Al forno

@L FOR-NO

Broiled

Alla graticola

@L-L@ GR@-TEE-KO-L@

Steamed

Al vapore

@L V@-PO-Rē

Fried

Fritto

FREET-TO

Rare

Al sangue

@L S@N-GWē

Medium

Cotta normale

KOT-T@ NOR-M@-Lē

Well done

Ben cotta

BēN KOT-T@

PROBLEMS

I didn't order this.

Non ho ordinato questo.

NON O OR-DEE-Nah-TO KWeS-TO

Is the bill correct?

Il conto è esatto?

EL KON-TO e e-Zah'T-TO

Please bring me...

Per favore, mi porti...

PeR Fah-VO'-Re ME POR-TEE

GETTING AROUND

Getting around in a foreign country can be an adventure in itself! Taxi (**Tassì**) and bus drivers do not always speak English, so it is essential to be able to give simple directions. The words and phrases in this chapter will help you get where you're going.

- The best way to get a taxi is at a taxi stand. Taxis have meters that are preset with different amounts depending on the time of day.

- Trains are used frequently by visitors to Europe. They are efficient and provide connections between large cities and towns throughout the country. Arrive early to allow time for ticket purchasing and checking in, and remember, trains leave on time!

- **Stazione della Metropolitana** or subway in Italy offers an easy way to get around. A red **"M"** usually indicates a subway stop.

- Check with your travel agent about special rail passes that allow unlimited travel within a set period of time.

KEY WORDS

Airport

Aeroporto

@-ⓔ-ℝⓄ-PⓄℝ-TⓄ

Bus Station / Bus Stop

Stazione dell'autobus

Fermata dell'autobus

STⓐ-TSⒺⒺ-Ⓞ-Nⓔ DⓔˈL ⓄⓌ-TⓄ-BⓄⓄS

Fⓔℝ-Mⓐ-Tⓐ DⓔˈL ⓄⓌ-TⓄ-BⓄⓄS

Car Rental Agency

Agenzia di autonoleggio

@-Jⓔ̃N-TSⒺⒺˈ-Yⓐ DⒺⒺ

ⓄⓌ-TⓄ-NⓄ-Lⓔˈ-CHⓄ

Subway Station

Stazione della metropolitana

STⓐ-TSⒺⒺ-Ⓞ-Nⓔ Dⓔˈ-Lⓐ

Mⓔ̃-TℝⓄ-PⓄ-LⒺⒺ-Tⓐˈ-Nⓐ

Taxi Stand

Posteggio di tassì

PⓄ-STⓔ̃ˈ-JⓄ DⒺⒺ Tⓐ̃S-SⒺⒺˈ

Train Station

Stazione ferroviaria

STⓐ-TSⒺⒺ-Ⓞ-Nⓔ Fⓔ̃-ℝⓄ-VⒺⒺ-ⓐˈ-ℝⒺⒺ-ⓐ

AIR TRAVEL

Arrivals	**Departures**
Arrivi	Partenze
ah-REE-VEE	PahR-TEN-TSe

Flight number

Numero di volo

NOO-ME-RO DEE VO-LO

Airline

Compagnia aerea

KOM-Pah-NEE-ah   ah-e-Re-ah

Gate

Cancello

KahN-CHeL-LO

Information

Informazione

EEN-FOR-Mah-TSEE-O-Ne

Ticket (airline)

Biglietto aereo

BEEL-YeT-TO   ah-e-Re-O

Reservations

Prenotazioni

PRe-NO-Tah-TSEE-O-NEE

PHRASEMAKER

I would like a seat…

Vorrei un posto…

VO-Rĕĕĕĕĕĕĕĕĕĕĕĕĕĕĕĕĕĕĕĕĕ

VO-Rĕ́-EE ooN POS-TO…

▸ **in first class**

in prima classe

EEN PRĔĔ-Mah KLahS-Sĕ

▸ **in the no-smoking section**

tra i non fumatori

TRah EE NoN Foo-Mah-TO-RĕĔ

▸ **next to the window**

accanto al finestrino

ahK-KahN-TO ahL FĔĔ-Nĕ́S-TRĔĔ-NO

▸ **on the aisle**

vicino al corridoio

VĔĔ-CHĔĔ-NO ahL KO-RĔĔ-DO-EE-O

▸ **near the exit**

vicino all'uscita

VĔĔ-CHĔĔ-NO ahL oo-SHĔĔ-Tah

BY BUS

Bus

Autobus

ⓐⓦ-Tⓞ-BⓞⓞS

Where is the bus stop?

Dov'è la fermata dell'autobus?

Dⓞ-Vⓔ̆ Lⓐ FⓔR-Mⓐ-Tⓐ

Dⓔ̆L ⓐⓦ-Tⓞ-BⓞⓞS

Do you go to…?

Va a…?

Vⓐ ⓐ…

What is the fare?

Quanto costa il biglietto?

KWⓐN-Tⓞ KⓞS-Tⓐ ⒺL BⒺⒺL-Yⓔ̆-Tⓞ

Do I need the exact amount?

Ho bisogno dell'ammontare esatto?

ⓞ BⒺⒺ-Zⓞ̆N-Yⓞ Dⓔ̆L

ⓐM-MⓞN-Tⓐ-Rⓔ̆ ⓔ̆-ZⓐT-Tⓞ

How often do the buses run?

Ogni quanti minuti passa l'autobus?

ⓞN-YⒺⒺ KWⓐN-TⒺⒺ MⒺⒺ-Nⓞⓞ-TⒺⒺ

Pⓐ̆S-Sⓐ Lⓞⓦ-Tⓞ-BⓞⓞS

PHRASEMAKER

Please tell me...

Per favore mi dica...

PĕR Fah-VŌ-Rĕ MĒĒ DĒĒ-Kah...

▸ **which bus goes to...**

quale autobus va a...

KWah-Lĕ ow-TŌ-Boos Vah ah...

▸ **what time the bus leaves**

a che ora parte l'autobus

ah KA Ō-Rah PahR-TA Low-TŌ-Boos

▸ **where the bus stop is**

dov'è la fermata dell'autobus

DŌ-Vĕ Lah FĕR-Mah-Tah DĕL ow-TŌ-Boos

▸ **when to get off**

quando devo scendere

KWahN-DŌ Dĕ-VŌ SHĕN-Dĕ-Rĕ

BY CAR

Fill it up.

Faccia il pieno.

F@h-CH@h EEL PEE-@-N⊙

Can you help me?

Può aiutarmi?

PW⊙ @h-Y⊙⊙-T@hR-MEE

My car won't start.

La mia auto non funziona.

L@h MEE-@h ⊙w-T⊙ N⊙N
F⊙⊙N-TSEE-⊙N-@h

Can you fix it?

Può aggiustarla?

PW⊙ @h-J⊙⊙S-T@hR-L@h

What will it cost me?

Quanto mi costerà?

KW@hN-T⊙ MEE K⊙S-T@-R@h

How long will it take?

Quanto tempo ci sarà?

KW@hN-T⊙ T@M-P⊙ CHEE S@h-R@h

PHRASEMAKER

Please check...

Potrebbe verificare... Per favore

PO-TRĕB-Bĕ VĕR-EE-FEE-Kah-Rĕ... PF

▶ **the battery**

la batteria

Lah Bah T-Tĕ-REE-ah

▶ **the brakes**

i freni

EE FRĕ-NEE

▶ **the oil**

l'olio

LO-L EE-O

▶ **the tires**

le gomme

Lĕ GOM-Mĕ

▶ **the water**

l'acqua

Lah-KWah

SUBWAYS AND TRAINS

Where is the subway station?

Dov'è la stazione della metropolitana?

DO-Vẽ Lah ST@h-TS€€-Ó-N€
Dẽ́L-L@h M€-TR̃O-PO-L€€-T@h́-N@h

Where is the train station?

Dov'è la stazione ferroviaria?

DO-Vẽ L@h ST@h-TS€€-Ó-N€
F€-R̃O-V€€-@h́-R̃€€-@h

A one-way ticket, please.

Un biglietto di sola andata, per favore.

©ON B€€L-Yẽ́T-TO D€€ SÓ-L@h
@h-D@h́-T@h P€R̃ F@h-VÓ-R̃€

A round trip ticket

Un biglietto d'andata e ritorno

©ON B€€L-Yẽ́-TO D@hN-D@h́-T@h
ẽ R̃€€-TÓR̃-NO

First class

Prima classe

PR̃€€́-M@h KL@h́S-S€

Second class

Seconda classe

S€̃-KÓN-D@h KL@h́S-S€

Which train do I take to go to…?

Quale treno devo prendere per andare a…?

KWah-Lĕ TRĕ-NO Dĕ-VO
PRĕN-Dĕ-Rĕ PĕR ahN-Dah-Rĕ ah...

What is the fare?

Quanto costa il biglietto?

KWahN-TO KOS-Tah EEL
BEEL-YĕT-TO

Is this seat taken?

Questo posto è occupato?

KWĕS-TO POS-TO ĕ
O-Koo-Pah-TO

Do I have to change trains?

Devo cambiar dei treni?

Dĕ-VO KahM-BEE-ahR
DĕEE TRĕ-NEE

Does this train stop at…?

Questo treno si ferma a…?

KWĕS-TO TRĕ-NO SEE FĕR-Mah ah...

Where are we?

Dove siamo?

DO-Vĕ SEE-ah-MO

TAXI

Can you call a taxi for me?

Potrebbe chiamarmi un tassì?

PO-TREB-BE KEE-ah-MahR-MEE
OON TaK-SEE

Are you available?

È libero?

E LEE-BE-RO

I want to go to…

Vorrei andare a...

VO-REE-EE ahN-Dah-RE ah...

Stop here, please.

Si fermi qui, per favore.

SEE FeR-MEE KWEE PF

Please wait for me.

Mi aspetti, per favore.

MEE ah-SPET-TEE PF

How much do I owe?

Quanto le devo?

KWahN-TO LE DE-VO

PHRASEMAKER

I would like to go…

Vorrei andare...

VO-RĕĒ-EE ahN-Dah-Rĕ...

▸ **to this address**

a questo indirizzo

ah KWĕS-TO EEN-DEE-RĕĒT-TSO

▸ **to the airport**

all'aeroporto

ahL ah ĕ-RO-POR-TO

▸ **to the bank**

alla banca.

ahL Lah BahN-Kah

▸ **to the hotel**

all'hotel

ahL O-TĕL

▸ **to the hospital**

all'ospedale

ahL OS-Pĕ-Dah-Lĕ

▸ **to the subway station**

alla stazione della metropolitana

ah-Lah STah-TSEE-O-Nĕ DĕL-Lah
Mĕ-TRO-PO-LEE-Tah-Nah

SHOPPING

Whether you plan a major shopping spree or just need to purchase some basic necessities, the following information is useful.

- Shops are usually open between 9 AM and 7 PM, closing two or three hours in the afternoon.

- I.V.A. (sales tax) rebate is available to tourists within 90 days of purchase. However, there is a minimum amount that must be spent and it must be in the same store in the same day.

- Always keep receipts for everything you buy! Your receipt must be stamped by Customs and mailed back to the vendor in order to qualify for a rebate.

SIGNS TO LOOK FOR:

FIORAIO (Florist)

FARMACIA (Pharmacy)

SUPERMERCATO (Supermarket)

GIOIELLERIA (Jewelry Store)

TABACCHERIA (Corner Store, stamps, newspaper, tickets, candy)

GELATERIA (Ice-cream store)

PANETTERIA (Bakery - Bread)

KEY WORDS

Credit card

Carta di credito

KaR-Tah DEE KREe-DEE-TO

Money

Denaro

DEe-Nah-RO

Receipt

Ricevuta

REE-CHEe-Voo-Tah

Sale

Vendita

VEeN-DEE-Tah

Store

Negozio

NEe-GO-TSEE-O

Traveler's checks

Traveler's checks

TRah-VEe-LEeRS CHEeKS

USEFUL PHRASES

Do you sell…?

Vende…?

VĔN-DĔ…

Do you have…?

Avete…?

ah-VĔ-TĔ…

I want to buy…

Vorrei comprare...

VO-RĔ-EE KOM-PRah-RĔ…

How much?

Quanto costa?

KWahN-TO KOS-Tah

When are the shops open?

Quando sono aperti i negozi?

KWahN-DO SO-NO ah-PĔR-TEE EE
NĔ-GOT-SEE

No, thank you.

No, grazie.

NO GRah-TSEE-ĕ

I´m just looking.

Sto solo guardando.

STO SO´-LO GW@B-D@N-DO

It's very expensive.

E'molto costoso.

ⓔ MOL-TO KOS-TO´-ZO

Could you give me a discount?

Potrebbe farmi uno sconto?

PO-TRⒺB-BⒺ F@R-MEE@-NO SKON-TO

I'll take it!

Lo prendo!

LO PRⒺN-DO

I'd like a receipt, please.

Vorrei la ricevuta, per favore.

VO-RⒺ´-EE L@ REE-CHⒺ-VOO´-T@ PF

I want to return this.

Vorrei restituire questo.

VO-RⒺ´-EE RⒺS-TEE-TOO-EE´-RⒺ
KWⒺS-TO

It doesn't fit.

Non è della mia misura.

NON ⓔ DⒺL-L@ MEE-@ MEE-SOO-R@

PHRASEMAKER

I'm looking for…

Sto cercando…

ST◎ CH◉R-K⒜N-D◎…

▶ **a bakery**

una panetteria

◎◎-N⒜ P⒜-N◉T-T◉-R⒠-⒜

▶ **a bank**

una banca

◎◎-N⒜ B⒜N-K⒜

▶ **a barber shop**

un barbiere

◎◎N B⒜R-B⒠-◉-R◉

▶ **a camera shop**

un negozio di macchine fotografiche

◎◎N N◉-G◎-TS⒠-◎ D⒠
M⒜-K⒠-N◉ F◎-T◎-GR⒜-F⒠-K◉

▶ **a hair salon**

un parrucchiere

◎◎N P⒜-R◎◎K-K⒠-◉-R◉

▶ **a pharmacy**

una farmacia

◎◎-N⒜ F⒜R-M⒜-CH⒠-⒜

PHRASEMAKER

Do you sell…

Vende…

VÉN-DÉ…

▸ **aspirin?**

aspirina?

ahS-PEE-REE-Nah

▸ **cigarettes?**

sigarette?

SEE-Gah-RÉT-TÉ

▸ **deodorant?**

deodorante?

DÉ-O-DO-Rahn-TÉ

▸ **dresses?**

abiti da donna?

ah-BEE-TEE Dah DON-Nah

▸ **film?**

rullini fotografici?

ROOL-LEE-NEE
FO-TO-GRah-FEE-CHEE

▶ **pantyhose?**

collant?

KOL-LahNT

▶ **perfume?**

profumo?

PRO-Foo-MO

▶ **razor blades?**

lamette?

Lah-MeT-Te

▶ **shampoo?**

shampoo?

SHahM-PO

▶ **shaving cream?**

crema da barba?

KRe-Mah Dah BahB-Bah

▶ **shirts?**

camicie?

Kah-MEE-CHe

▶ **soap?**

di sapone?

DEE Sah-PO-Ne

▸ **sunglasses?**

occhiali da sole?

OK-KEE-ah-LEE Dah SO-Lĕ

▸ **sunscreen?**

crema antisolare?

KRĕ-Mah ahN-TEE-SO-Lah-Rĕ

▸ **toothbrushes?**

spazzolino da denti?

SPah T-TSO-LEE-NO DA DĕN-TEE

▸ **toothpaste?**

dentifricio?

DĕN-TEE-FRĕ-CHO

▸ **water?** (bottled)

bottiglie d'acqua?

BOT-TĕE-LYEE-ĕ Dah-KWah

▸ **water?** (mineral)

acqua minerale?

ah-KWah MEE-Nĕ-Rah-Lĕ

ESSENTIAL SERVICES

THE BANK

As a traveler in a foreign country your primary contact with banks will be to exchange money. Keep in mind that many banks close in the afternoon and on Saturday and Sunday.

- The Italian national currency is the euro. Bank notes are in denominations of € 500, 200, 100, 50, 20, 10, and 5. Coins are in denominations of € 2 and 1, and € 50, 20, 10, 5, 2, and 1 cents.

- Change enough funds before leaving home to pay for tips, food, and transportation to your final destination.

- Generally, you will receive a better rate of exchange at a bank, but rates can change from bank to bank. Exchange offices are found at airports, some train stations, and tourist sites.

- Current exchange rates are posted in banks and published daily in city newspapers.

- ATM machines are readily available. In Italy, they are known as **Bancomat**. Traveler's checks and credit cards are accepted in most major tourist cities.

KEY WORDS

Bank

Banca

BahN-Kah

Exchange office

Ufficio di cambio

oo-FEE-CHO DEE KahM-BEE-O

Money

Denaro

DĕN-Nah-RO

Money order

Mandato di pagamento

MahN-Dah-TO DEE
Pah-Gah-MĕN-TO

Traveler's checks

Traveler's checks

TRah-VĕL-LĕRS CHĕKS

USEFUL PHRASES

Where is the bank?

Dov'è la banca?

DO-VĕĚ Lah Bah'N-Kah

What time does the bank open?

A che ora apre la banca?

ah Kĕ O-Rah ah-PRĕ
Lah Bah'N-Kah

Where is the exchange office?

Dov'è l'ufficio di cambio?

DO-VĕĚ Loo-FĕĚ-CHO DĔĔ
Kah'M-BĔĔ-O

What time does the exchange office open?

A che ora apre l'ufficio di cambio?

ah Kĕ O-Rah ah-PRĕ
Loo-FĕĚ-CHO DĔĔ Kah'M-BĔĔ-O

Can I change dollars here?

Posso cambiare i dollari qui?

POS-SO Kah'M-BĔĔ-ah-Rĕ ĔĔ
DOL-Lah-RĔĔ KWĔĔ

Can you change this?

Può cambiarmi questo?

PW⊙ KⓐM-B⒠-ⓐʀ-M⒠ KW⒠S-T⊙

What is the exchange rate?

Qual'è il cambio?

KWⓐ-L⒠ ⒠L KⓐM-B⒠-⊙

I would like large bills.

Vorrei banconote di grosso taglio.

V⊙-ʀ⒠-⒠ BⓐN-K⊙-N⊙-T⒠ D⒠
GʀⓄS-S⊙ TⓐL-Y⊙

I would like small bills.

Vorrei banconote di meno taglio.

V⊙-ʀ⒠-⒠ BⓐN-K⊙-N⊙-T⒠ D⒠
M⒠-N⊙ TⓐL-Y⊙

I need change. (coins)

Ho bisogno moneta riccola.

⊙ B⒠-Z⊙N-Y⊙ M⊙-N⒠-T⒠
ʀ⒠-K⊙-Lⓐ

Do you have an ATM?

Avete un bancomat?

ⓐ-V⒠-T⒠ ⓄN BⓐN-K⊙-MⓐT

POST OFFICE

POSTE E TELECOMUNI-CAZIONI or **PT** identify the post office. Stamps can be purchased at a **tabaccheria** as well as in certain cafés and post offices.

KEY WORDS

Airmail

Via aerea

VEE´-ah ah-E´-REE-ah

Letter

Lettera

LE´T-TE-Rah

Post office

Ufficio postale

OO-FEE´-CHO POS-Tah´-LA

Postcard

Cartolina postale

KahR-TO-LEE´-Nah POS-Tah´-LA

Stamps

Francobolli

FRahN-KO-BOL´-LEE

USEFUL PHRASES

Where is the post office?

Dov'è l'ufficio postale?

DO-Vĕ́ LOO-FĒE-CHO POS-Tah-Lĕ

What time does the post office open?

A che ora apre l'ufficio postale?

ah Kĕ oo-Rah ah-PRĕ
LOO-FĒE-CHO POS-Tah-Lĕ

I need stamps.

Ho bisogno di francobolli.

O BĒE-ZON-YO DĒE
FRah-N-KO-BOOL-LĒE

I need an envelope.

Ho bisogno d'una busta.

O BĒE-ZON-YO DOO-Nah BOOS-Tah

I need a pen.

Ho bisogno d'una penna.

O BĒE-ZON-YO DOO-Nah PAN-Nah

TELEPHONE

Placing phone calls in a foreign
country can be a test of will and
stamina! Besides the obvious
language barriers, service can vary greatly from
one town to the next.

- In Italy, phone calls can be made from the post
  office, especially long-distance calls.

- It is a good idea to purchase a phone card on
  arrival in Italy at the airport or train station.
  Newsstands and tobacco shops also sell
  phone cards.

- **Tabaccheria** is the local corner store where
  you can purchase phone cards, newspapers,
  stamps, tickets, candy, etc.

- Long-distance calls can be dialed on public
  telephones. Most use phone cards. When you
  use a phone card, you will reach an operator
  who speaks the language of the destination
  call.

KEY WORDS

Information
Informazione

ⒺN-FⓄB-Mⓐ-TSⒺ-Ⓞ-Nⓔ

Long distance
Interurbano

ⒺN-Tⓔ-BⓄB-Bⓐ-NⓄ

Operator
Signorina / Centralino

SⒺN-YⓄ-BⒺ-Nⓐ /

CHⓔN-TBⓐ-LⒺ-NⓄ

Phone book
Elenco telefonica

ⓔ-LⓔN-KⓄ Tⓔ-Lⓔ-FⓄ-NⒺ-Kⓐ

Public telephone
Telefono pubblico

Tⓔ-Lⓔ-FⓄ-NⓄ PⓄB-BLⒺ-KⓄ

Telephone
Telefono

Tⓔ-Lⓔ-FⓄ-NⓄ

USEFUL PHRASES

May I use your telephone?

Posso usare il suo telefono?

PO'S-SO   oo-Zah-Re   EL

Soo-O   Te-Le-FO-NO

I don't speak Italian.

Non parlo italiano.

NON   Pah'R-LO   EE-Tah-LEE-ah-NO

I would like to make a call long distance.

Vorrei fare una telefonata interurbana.

VO-Re'-EE   Fah-Re   oo'-Nah

TA-LA-FO-Nah'-Tah

EEN-Te-ROOB-Bah'-Nah

I would like to make a call to the United States.

Vorrei fare una telefonata agli Stati Uniti.

VO-Re'-EE   Fah-Re   oo'-Nah

TA-LA-FO-Nah'-Tah   ah'L-YEE

STah'-TEE   oo-NEE'-TEE

I want to call this number...

Vorrei chiamare questo numero...

VO-R̃ẽ́-EE KEE-ah-M@h́-R̃ẽ
KW@S-TO NOO-Mẽ-RO...

1 uno OO-NO	**2** due DOO-ẽ	**3** tre TR̃ẽ
4 quattro KW@h-TR̃O	**5** cinque CHEEN-KWẽ	**6** sei Sẽ-EE
7 sette Sẽ́T-Tẽ	**8** otto ÓT-TO	**9** nove NÓ-Vẽ
	0 zero Zẽ́-R̃O	**#**

SIGHTSEEING AND ENTERTAINMENT

In most towns in Italy you will find tourist information offices. Here you can usually obtain brochures, maps, historical information, bus and train schedules.

There are many ways to discover Italy from concerts, plays, and festivals to beautiful open-air squares and streets. Visit beautiful churches, palaces, monuments, castles, and museums or just relax and enjoy a cappuccino or glass of wine!

ITALIAN CITIES

Roma (Rome)
RŌ-Mah

Napoli (Naples)
Nah-PŌ-LEE

Milano (Milan)
MEE-Lah-NŌ

Pisa (Pisa)
PEE-Zah

Venezia (Venice)
Vĕ-NĕT-SEE-ah

Firenze (Florence)
FEE-RĕN-TSĕ

KEY WORDS

Admission

Entrata

ⓔN-TⓇⓐh-Tⓐh

Map

Cartina

KⓐhⓇ-TⒺⒺ-Nⓐh

Reservation

Prenotazione

PⓇⓔ-NⓄ-Tⓐh-TSⒺⒺ-Ⓞ-Nⓔ

Ticket

Biglietto

BⒺⒺL-YⓔT-TⓄ

Tour

Viaggio / Gita

VⒺⒺ-ⓐh-JⓄ / JⒺⒺ-Tⓐh

Tour guide

Guida turistica

GWⒺⒺ-Dⓐh TⓄⓄ-ⓇⒺⒺS-TⒺⒺ-Kⓐh

USEFUL PHRASES

Where is the tourist office?

Dov'è l'ufficio turistico?

DŌ-Vĕ̃ LŌ-FĒ-CHŌ
TOO-RĔ̃S-TĒ-KŌ

Is there a tour to…?

Avete un giro turistico per…?

ah-Vĕ̃-Tĕ̃ OON JĒ-RŌ
TOO-RĔ̃S-TĒ-KŌ PĕR…

Where do I buy a ticket for…?

Dove posso comprare un biglietto per…

DŌ-Vĕ̃ PŌS-SO KŌM-PRah-Rĕ̃
OON BĒL-Yĕ̃-TO PĕR…

How much does the tour cost?

Quanto costa il giro turistico?

KWahN-TO KŌS-Tah ĒL
JĒ-RŌ TOO-RĔ̃S-TĒ-KŌ

How long does the tour take?

Quanto dura il giro turistico?

KWahN-TO DOO-Rah ĒL
JĒ-RŌ TOO-RĔ̃S-TĒ-KŌ

Does the guide speak English?

La guida parla inglese?

Lah GWEE-Dah PahR-Lah EEN-GLĕ-Zĕ

Do children pay?

I bambini pagano?

EE BahM-BEE-NEE Pah-Gah-NO

What time does the show start?

A che ora comincia lo spettacolo?

ah KA Ó-Rah KO-MEEN-CHah

LO SPĕT-Tah-KO-LO

Do I need reservations?

E' necessaria la prenotazione?

A NA-CHA-Sah-REE-ah Lah

PRA-NO-Tah-TSEE-Ó-NA

Where can we go dancing?

Dove si può andare a ballare?

DÓ-Vĕ SEE PWO ahN-Dah-Rĕ

ah BahL-Lah-Rĕ

Is there a minimum cover charge?

C'è un prezzo minimo?

CHĕ ooN PRĕT-TSO MEE-NEE-MO

PHRASEMAKER

May I invite you...

Posso invitarti...

PⓄS-SⓄ ⒺN-VⒺ-TⓐʜR-TⒺ...

▶ **to a concert?**

a un concerto?

ⓐʜ ⓄⓄN KⓄN-CHⒺʜR-TⓄ

▶ **to dance?**

a ballare?

ⓐʜ BⓐʜL-LⓐʜR-RⒺ

▶ **to dinner?**

a pranzo?

ⓐʜ PʀⓐʜN-TSⓄ

▶ **to the movies?**

al cinema?

ⓐʜL CHⒺ-NⒺ-Mⓐʜ

▶ **to the theater?**

al teatro?

ⓐʜL TⒺ-ⓐʜ-TʀⓄ

PHRASEMAKER

Where can I find...

Dove posso trovare...

DŌ´-Vĕ PŌ´S-SŌ TRŌ-Vȧ´-Rĕ...

▶ **a health club?**

un club ginnico?

ⓞⓞN KLⓞⓞB JĒN-NĒ´-KⓄ

▶ **a swimming pool?**

una piscina?

ⓞⓞ´-Nȧ PĒE-SHĒE´-Nȧ

▶ **a tennis court?**

un campo da tennis?

ⓞⓞN Kȧ´M-PⓄ Dȧ TĒ´N-NĒES

▶ **a golf course?**

un campo di golf?

ⓞⓞN Kȧ´M-PⓄ DĒE GⓄLF

HEALTH

Hopefully you will not need medical attention on your trip. If you do, it is important to communicate basic information regarding your condition.

- Check with your insurance company before leaving home to find out if you are covered in a foreign country. You may want to purchase traveler's insurance before leaving home.

- If you take prescription medicine, carry your prescription with you. Have your prescriptions translated before you leave home.

- Take a small first-aid kit with you.

- Your embassy or consulate should be able to assist you in finding health care.

- Pharmacies are open in the morning and usually from 3:30 PM till 7:30 PM.

- Medical facilities and public hospitals are available in Italy. However, you may want to check your insurance for coverage for care or stay in a private Italian hospital or clinic.

KEY WORDS

Ambulance

Ambulanza

ahM-Boo-Lah'N-TSah

Dentist

Dentista

DĕN-TEE'S-Tah

Doctor

Medico

Mĕ'-DEE-KO

Emergency!

Emergenza!

ĕ-MĕR-JĕN-TSah

Hospital

Ospedale

OS-Pĕ-Dah'-Lĕ

Prescription

Ricetta

REE-CHĕ'T-Tah

USEFUL PHRASES

I am sick.

Sono ammalato. (male)

SŌ-NO ⓐⓗM-Mⓐⓗ-Lⓐⓗ-TO

I am sick.

Sono ammalata. (female)

SŌ-NO ⓐⓗM-Mⓐⓗ-Lⓐⓗ-Tⓐⓗ

I need a doctor.

Ho bisogno di un dottore.

Ⓞ Bⓔⓔ-ZŌN-YO Dⓔⓔ ⓞⓞN DOT-TŌ-Bⓔ

It's an emergency!

È un'emergenza!

ⓔ̆ ⓞⓞN ⓔ̆-Mⓔ̆R-Jⓔ̆N-Sⓐⓗ

Where is the nearest hospital?

Dov'è l'ospedale più vicino?

DŌ-Vⓔ̆ LⓄS-Pⓔ̆-Dⓐⓗ-Lⓔ̆

Pⓔⓔ-ⓞⓞ Vⓔⓔ-CHⓔⓔ-NO

Call an ambulance!

Chiamate un'ambulanza!

Kⓔⓔ-ⓐⓗ-Mⓐⓗ-Tⓔ̆ ⓞⓞN ⓐⓗM-Bⓞⓞ-LⓐⓗN-TSⓐⓗ

I'm allergic to…

Sono allergico a...

SO̱-NO̱ ah-L-L-e̱R-JEE-KO̱ ah…

I'm pregnant.

Sono incinta.

SO̱-NO̱ EEN-CHEEN-Tah

I'm diabetic.

Sono diabetico. (male) Sono diabetica. (female)

SO̱-NO̱ DEE-ah-Be̱-TEE-KO̱ (Kah)

I have a heart condition.

Sono debole di cuore.

SO̱-NO̱ De̱-BO-Le̱ DEE KWO̱-Re̱

I have high blood pressure.

Ho la pressione alta.

O̱ Lah PRe̱S-SEE-O̱-Ne̱ aẖL-Tah

I have low blood pressure.

Ho la pressione bassa.

O̱ Lah PRe̱S-SEE-O̱-Ne̱ BaẖS-Sah

PHRASEMAKER

I need…

Ho bisogno di...

Ⓞ BⒺⒺ-ZⓄⓄ′N-YⓄ DⒺⒺ...

▶ **a doctor**

un medico

ⓄⓄN MⒺ́-DⒺⒺ-KⓄ

▶ **a dentist**

un dentista

ⓄⓄN DⒺ̃N-TⒺⒺ′S-Tⓐⓗ

▶ **a nurse**

un'infermiera

ⓄⓄN ⒺⒺN-FⒺ̃R-MⒺⒺ-Ⓔ̃-Rⓐⓗ

▶ **an optician**

un ottico

ⓄⓄN Ⓞ́T-TⒺⒺ-KⓄ

▶ **a pharmacist**

un farmacista

ⓄⓄN FⓐⓗR-Mⓐⓗ-CHⒺⒺ′S-Tⓐⓗ

PHRASEMAKER

(AT THE PHARMACY)

Do you have…

Avete...

ⓐ-Vⓔ́-Tⓔ...

▸ **aspirin?**

aspirina?

ⓐS-PⒺ-RⒺ́-Nⓐ

▸ **Band-Aids?**

cerotti?

CHⓔ-RⓄ́T-TⒺ

▸ **cough medicine?**

sciroppo per la tosse?

SHⒺ-RⓄ́P-PⓄ PⓔR Lⓐ TⓄ́S-Sⓔ

▸ **ear drops?**

gocce per le orecchie?

GⓄ́-CHⓔ PⓔR Lⓔ Ⓞ-Rⓔ́-KⒺ-ⓔ

▸ **eyedrops?**

collirio?

KⓄL-LⒺ-RⒺ́-Ⓞ

BUSINESS TRAVEL

It is important to show appreciation and interest in another person's language and culture, particularly when doing business. A few well-pronounced phrases can make a great impression.

I have an appointment.

Ho un appuntamento.

Ⓞ ⓄⓄN ⒶP-PⓄⓄN-Tⓐⓗ-MⒺⓃ-TⓄ

Here is my card.

Ecco il mio biglietto da visita.

ⒺK-KⓄ ⒺL MⒺⒺ-Ⓞ BⒺⒺL-YⒺ-TⓄ Dⓐⓗ VⒺⒺ-ZⒺⒺ-Tⓐⓗ

I need an interpreter?

Ho bisogno d'interprete?

Ⓞ BⒺⒺ-ZⓄN-YⓄ DⒺⒺN-TⒺⓇ-PⓇⒶ-TⒺ

May I speak to Mr....?

Posso parlare con il signor...?

PⓄS-SⓄ PⓐⓗⓇ-Lⓐⓗ-ⓇⒶ KⓄN ⒺL SⒺⒺN-YⓄR...

May I speak to Mrs...?

Posso parlare con la signora...?

PⓄS-SⓄ PⓐⓗⓇ-Lⓐⓗ-ⓇⒶ KⓄN Lⓐⓗ SⒺⒺN-YⓄ-Ⓡⓐⓗ...

KEY WORDS

Appointment

Appuntamento

@P-P∞N-T@-M@N-T©

Meeting

Incontro

@N-K©N-TR©

Marketing

Marketing

M@R-K@-T@N

Presentation

Presentazione

PR@-Z@N-T@-TS@-©-N@

Sales

Vendite

V@N-D@-T@

PHRASEMAKER

I need…

Ho bisogno di...

Ⓞ Bⓔ-ZⓄN-YⓄ Dⓔ...

▸ **a computer**

un computer

ⓞN KⓄM-PYⓞ-TⓔR

▸ **a copy machine**

una fotocopiatrice

ⓞ-Nⓐ FⓄ-TⓄ-KⓄ-Pⓔ-ⓐ-TRⓔ-CHⓔ

▸ **a conference room**

una sala conferenze

ⓞ-Nⓐ Sⓐ-Lⓐ
KⓄN-Fⓔ-Bⓔ N-TSⓔ

▸ **a fax machine**

una macchina per fax

ⓞ-Nⓐ Mⓐ-Kⓔ-Nⓐ PⓔR Fⓐ KS

▸ **an interpreter**

un interprete

ⓞN ⓔN-TⓔR-PBⓐ-Tⓔ

▸ **a lawyer**

un avvocato

ⓄⓄN ⓐⓗV-VⓄ-Kⓐⓗ-TⓄ

▸ **a notary**

un notaio

ⓄⓄN NⓄ-Tⓐⓗ-YⓄ

▸ **overnight delivery**

un recapito urgente

ⓄⓄN Rⓔ-Kⓐⓗ-Pⓔⓔ-TⓄ ⓄⓄR-Jⓔ́N-Tⓔ

▸ **paper**

carta

KⓐⓗR-Tⓐⓗ

▸ **a pen**

una penna

ⓄⓄ-Nⓐⓗ Pⓐ́N-Nⓐⓗ

▸ **a pencil**

una matita

ⓄⓄ-Nⓐⓗ Mⓐⓗ-Tⓔⓔ-Tⓐⓗ

▸ **a secretary**

una segretaria

ⓄⓄ-Nⓐⓗ Sⓔ́G-Rⓔ-TⓐⓗR-Yⓐⓗ

GENERAL INFORMATION

From warm summers and cool winters in the north and hot summers and mild winters in southern Italy, there is something for everyone!

THE SEASONS

Spring

La primavera

Lah PREE-Mah-Vē-Rah

Summer

L'estate

Lēs-Tah-Tē

Autumn

L'autunno

Low-Toon-No

Winter

L'inverno

Leen-Vēr-No

THE DAYS

Monday
lunedì
L👓-Nê-Deé

Tuesday
martedì
Mah-R-Tê-Deé

Wednesday
mercolidì
Mê-R-KO-Lê-Deé

Thursday
giovedì
JO-Vê-Deé

Friday
venerdì
Vê-Nê-R-Deé

Saturday
sabato
Sah-Bah-TO

Sunday
domenica
DO-Mê-Nee-Kah

THE MONTHS

January
gennaio
JEN-Nah-YO

February
febbraio
FEB-BRah-YO

March
marzo
Mah-R-TSO

April
aprile
ah-PREE-Le

May
maggio
Mah-JO

June
giugno
JOON-YO

July
luglio
LOOL-YO

August
agosto
ah-GOS-TO

September
settembre
SET-TEM-BRe

October
ottobre
OT-TO-BRe

November
novembre
NO-VEM-BRe

December
dicembre
DEE-CHEM-BRe

COLORS

Black	**White**
Nero	Bianco
NĔ-RO	BEE-ăN-KO
Blue	**Brown**
Blu	Marrone
BLoo	Măh-RO-NĔ
Gray	**Gold**
Grigio	Oro
GREE-JO	O-RO
Orange	**Yellow**
Arancione	Giallo
ăh-Răn-CHO-NĔ	JEE-ăL-LO
Red	**Green**
Rosso	Verde
RO-S-SO	VĔR-DĔ
Pink	**Purple**
Rosa	Porpora
RO-Zăh	POR-PO-Răh

NUMBERS

0	1	2
zero	uno	due
Zĕ-RO	◎́-NO	D◎́-ĕ

3	4	5
tre	quattro	cinque
TRĕ	KWⓐT-TRO	CHēN-KWĕ

6	7	8
sei	sette	otto
Sĕē	Sĕ́T-Tĕ	◎́T-TO

9	10	11
nove	dieci	undici
N◎-Vĕ	Dē-ĕ́-CHē	◎N-Dē-CHē

12	13
dodici	tredici
D◎́-Dē-CHē	TRĕ́-Dē-CHē

14	15
quattordici	quindici
KWⓐT-T◎R-Dē-CHē	KWēN-Dē-CHē

16	17
sedici	diciassette
Sĕ́-Dē-CHē	Dē-CH ⓐS-Sĕ́T-Tĕ

18
diciotto
DEE-CHOT-TO

19
diciannove
DEE-CHahN-NO-Vĕ

20
venti
VĕN-TEE

30
trenta
TRĕN-Tah

40
quaranta
KWah-Rah-N-Tah

50
cinquanta
CHEEN-KWahN-Tah

60
sessanta
Sĕ-SahN-Tah

70
settanta
SĕT-TahN-Tah

80
ottanta
OT-TahN-Tah

90
novanta
NO-VahN-Tah

100
cento
CHĕN-TO

1000
mille
MEEL-Lĕ

1,000,000
milione
MEEL-YO-Nĕ

ITALIAN VERBS

Verbs are the action words of any language. In Italian there are three main types; **–are**, **–ere**, and **–ire**.

The foundation form for all verbs is called the infinitive. This is the form you will find in dictionaries. In English, we place "to" in front of the verb name to give us the infinitive; e.g., to sing. In Italian, the **infinito** is one word. For example, **cantare**, means by itself to sing, and (as in English) it does not change its form.

On the following pages you will see the present tense conjugation of the three regular verb groups: **–are**, **–ere**, and **–ire**. Conjugating a verb is what you do naturally in your own language: *I sing, he sees, they sleep*. A verb is called regular when it follows one of these three models: its basic form does not change, just the endings that correspond to the subject of the verb.

In your study of Italian, you will come across irregular verbs and verbs with spelling changes. Their conjugation will require memorization. However, the Phrasemaker on page 128 will help you avoid this problem. First choose a form of "want," then select an infinitive; 150 are provided in the following section. And because the infintive does not change, you don't need to worry about the conjugation of the verb or whether it is regular or irregular!

-ARE VERB CONJUGATION

Find below the present tense conjugation for the regular
–ARE verb **cantare**, meaning **to sing**. The English
equivalent is: *I sing* (or *I am singing*), *you sing* (*you are
singing*), etc. For regular **-ARE** verbs like this, drop the
infinitive ending and add **-o**, **-i**, **-a**, **-iamo**, **-ate** or **-ano**.

I sing.

Io cant**o**.

EE-O KahN-TO

You sing. (informal)

Tu cant**i**.

TOO KahN-TEE

He sings. / She sings. / You sing. (formal)

Lui cant**a**. / Lei cant**a**. / Lei cant**a**.

LOO-E KahN-Tah / LE-EE KahN-Tah

We sing.

Noi cant**iamo**.

NOY KahN-TEE-ah-MO

You sing (plural)

Voi cant**ate**.

VOY KahN-Tah-TEE

They sing

Loro cant**ano**.

LO-RO KahN-Tah-NO

–ERE VERB CONJUGATION

Find below the present tense conjugation for the regular
–ERE verb **vedere**, meaning **to see**. The English equivalent
is: *I see* (or *I am seeing*), *you see* (*you are seeing*), etc.
For regular **–ERE** verbs like this, drop the infinitive ending
and add **-o**, **-i**, **-e**, **-iamo**, **-ete** or **-ono**.

I see.

Io ved**o**.

Ⓔ-Ⓞ VⒺ́-DⒺ

You see. (informal)

Tu ved**i**.

TⓄ VⒺ́-DⒺ

He sees. / She sees. / You see. (formal)

Lui ved**e** / Lei ved**e** / Lei ved**e**.

LⓄ́-Ⓔ VⒺ́-DⒺ / LⒺ́-Ⓔ VⒺ́-DⒺ

We see.

Noi ved**iamo**.

NⓄ VⒺ́-DⒺ-ⓐ́-MⓄ

You see. (plural)

Voi ved**ete**.

VⓄ VⒺ́-DⒺ́-TⒺ

They see.

Loro ved**ono**.

LⓄ́-RⓄ VⒺ́-DⓄ-NⓄ

–IRE VERB CONJUGATION

Find below the present tense conjugation for the regular **–IRE** verb **dormire**, meaning **to sleep**. The English equivalent is: *I sleep* (or *I am sleeping*), *you sleep* (*you are sleeping*), etc. For regular **–IRE** verbs like this, drop the infinitive ending and add -**o**, -**i**, -**e**, -**iamo**, -**ite** or -**ono**.

I sleep.

Io dorm**o**.

EE-O DOR-MO

You sleep. (informal)

Tu dorm**i**.

TOO DOR-MEE

He / she sleeps. / You sleep. (formal)

Lui dorm**e** / Lei dorm**e** / Lei dorm**e**.

LOO-E DOR-ME / LE-EE DOR-ME

We sleep.

Noi dorm**iamo**.

NOY DOR-MEE-ah-MO

You sleep. (plural)

Voi dorm**ite**.

VOY DOR-MEE-TE

They sleep.

Loro dorm**ono**.

LORO DOR-MO-NO

PHRASEMAKER

I want...

Io voglio...

Ⓔ-Ⓞ VⓄL-YⓄ...

You want...

Tu vuoi... (informal)

Tⓞⓞ VWⓞy-ⒺⒺ...

> It is easy to recognize Italian verbs in their infinitive form because they always end in **–are**, **–ere**, or **–ire**!

Lei vuole...(formal)

LⒺ-ⒺⒺ VWⓄ-LⒺ.

He wants...

Lui vuole...

Lⓞⓞ-ⒺⒺ VWⓄ-LⒺ.

◄ ▸ **to sing**

cant**are**

KⓐN-Tⓐh-RⒺ

She wants...

Lei voule...

LⒺ-ⒺⒺ VWⓄ-LⒺ.

◄ ▸ **to see**

ved**ere**

VⒺ-DⒺ-RⒺ

We want...

Noi vogliamo...

Nⓞy VⓞyⓁ-ⒺⒺ-ⓐh-M

◄ ▸ **to sleep**

dom**ire**

DⓄ-MⒺⒺ-RⒺ

They want...

Loro vogliono...

LⓄ-RⓄ VⓞyⓁ-ⒺⒺ-Ⓞ

150 VERBS

Here are some essential verbs that will carry you a long way towards learning Italian with the EPLS Vowel Symbol System!

to add

aggiungere

@G-GooN-Gĕ-Rĕ

to allow

permettere

PĕR-MĕT-Tĕ-Rĕ

to answer

rispondere

RĕS-PŏN-Dĕ-Rĕ

to arrive

arrivare

@-Rĕ-Vah-Rĕ

to ask

chiedere

Kĕ-ĕ-Dĕ-Rĕ

to attack

attacare

@T-Tah-Kah-Rĕ

to attend

assistere

@S-Sĕ-Tĕ-Rĕ

to bake

infornare

ĕN-FŏR-Nah-Rĕ

to be

essere

ĕS-Sĕ-Rĕ

to be able

potere

Pŏ-Tĕ-Rĕ

to beg

chiedere

Kĕĕ-Dĕ-Rĕ

to begin

cominciare

KŏM-MĕN-CHah-Rĕ

to believe

credere

KRĒ-DĒ-RĔ

to bother

molestare

MO-LĔS-Tah-RĔ

to break

rompere

ROM-PĔ-RĔ

to breathe

respirare

RĔS-PĒ-Rah-RĔ

to bring

portare

POR-Tah-RĔ

to build

construire

KON-STRoo-ĒE-RĔ

to burn

bruciare

BRoo-CHah-RĔ

to buy

comprare

KOM-PRah-RĔ

to call

chiamare

KĒE-ah-Mah-RĔ

to cancel

cancellare

Kah-CHĔ-Lah-RĔ

to carry

portare

POR-Tah-RĔ

to change

cambiare

Kah-M-BĒE-ah-RĔ

to chew

masticare

Mah-S-TĒE-Kah-RĔ

to clean

pulire

Poo-LĒE-RĔ

to climb	**to dance**
salire	balare
S@h-L㉤-R㉤	B@h-L@h-R㉤
to close	**to decide**
chiudere	decidere
K㊫-D㉤-R㉤	D㉤-CH㉤-D㉤-R㉤
to come	**to depart**
venire	partire
V㉤-N㉤-R㉤	P@hB-T㉤-R㉤
to cook	**disturb**
cucinare	disturbare
K㊫-CH㉤-N@h-R㉤	D㉤S-T㊫B-B@h-R㉤
to count	**to do**
contare	fare
K㋍N-T@h-R㉤	F@h-R㉤
to cry	**to drink**
piangere	bere
P㉤-@hN-J㉤-R㉤	B㉤-R㉤
to cut	**to drive**
tagliare	guidare
T@h-L㉤-@h-R㉤	GW㉤-D@h-R㉤

to dry

asciugare

ah-SHOO-Gah-Rē

to earn

guadagnare

GWah-Dah-NYah-Rē

to eat

mangiare

Mah N-Jah-Rē

to enjoy

godere

GO-Dē-Rē

to enter

entrare

ēN-TRah-Rē

to explain

spiegare

SPēē-ē-Gah-Rē

to feel

sentire

Sē N-Tēē-Rē

to fight

litigare

Lēē-Tēē-Gah-Rē

to fill

riempire

Rēē-ēM-Pēē-Rē

to find

trovare

TRO-Vah-Rē

to finish

finire

Fēē-Nēē-Rē

to fix

aggiustare

ah J-JOOS-Tah-Rē

to fly

volare

VO-Lah-Rē

to follow

seguire

Sē-GWēē-Rē

to forgive

perdonare

PĔR-DŌN-Nah'-Rĕ

to get

ottenere

ŌT-TĔN-ĕ'-Rĕ

to give

dare

Dah'-Rĕ

to go

andare

ahN-Dah'-Rĕ

to greet

salutare

Sah-Lōō-Tah'-Rĕ

to happen

succedere

Sōō-CHĕ'-Dĕ-Rĕ

to have

avere

ah-Vĕ'-Rĕ

to hear

ascoltare

ahS-KŌL-Tah'-Rĕ

to help

aiutare

ah-Yōō-Tah'-Rĕ

to hide

nascondere

Nah S-KŌN-Dĕ'-Rĕ

to hit

colpire

KŌL-PĔE-Rĕ

to imagine

imaginare

EE-Mah-JEE-Nah'-Rĕ

to improve

migliorare

MEE-LEE-Ō-Rah'-Rĕ

to judge

giudicare

Jōō-DEE-Kah'-Rĕ

to jump

saltire

S@L-T℮℮-R℮

to kiss

baciare

B@-CH@-R℮

to know

sapere

S@-P℮-R℮

to laugh

ridere

R℮℮-D℮-R℮

to learn

imparare

℮℮M-P@-R@-R℮

to leave

lasciare

L@-SH@-R℮

to lie (not the truth)

bugiare

B℮℮-J@-R℮

to lift

levare

L℮-V@-R℮

to like

piacere

P℮℮-@-CH℮-R℮

to listen

ascoltare

@S-K℮L-T@-R℮

to live

vivere

V℮℮-V℮-R℮

to look

vedere

V℮-D℮-R℮

to lose

perdere

P℮R-D℮-R℮

to love

amare

@-M@-R℮

to make
fare
F@ĥ-R⒠

to measure
misurare
M⒠-Z⓪⓪-R@ĥ-R⒠

to miss
mancare
M@ĥN-K@ĥ-R⒠

to move
muovere
MW⓪-V⒠-R⒠

to need
abbisognare
@ĥB-B⒠-Z⓪-NY@ĥ-R⒠

to offer
offrire
⓪F-FR⒠-R⒠

to open
aprire
@ĥP-R⒠-R⒠

to order
ordinare
⓪R-D⒠-N@ĥ-R⒠

to pack
impaccare

⒠M-P@ĥK-K@ĥ-R⒠

to pass (object or time)
passare
P@ĥS-S@ĥ-R⒠

to pay
pagare
P@ĥ-G@ĥ-R⒠

to play
giocare
J⓪-K@ĥ-R⒠

to pretend
pretendere
PR⒠-T⒠N-D⒠-R⒠

to print
imprimere
⒠M-PR⒠-M⒠-R⒠

to promise

prometere

PR⊙-M⊛-T⊛-R⊛

to pronounce

pronunciare

PR⊙-N⊙⊙N-CH⊛-R⊛

to push

spingere

SP⊛N-J⊛-R⊛

to put

mettere

M⊛T-T⊛-R⊛

to quit

smettere

TSM⊛T-T⊛-R⊛

to read

leggere

L⊛J-J⊛-R⊛

to receive

ricevere

R⊛-CH⊛-V⊛-R⊛

to recommend

raccomandare

R⊛K-K⊙-M⊛N-D⊛-R⊛

to remember

ricordare

R⊛-K⊙R-D⊛-R⊛

to rent

affittare

⊛F-F⊛T-T⊛-R⊛

to rescue

salvare

S⊛L-V⊛-R⊛

to rest

riposare

R⊛-P⊙-Z⊛-R⊛

to return

ritornare

R⊛-T⊙R-N⊛-R⊛

to run

correre

K⊙R-R⊛-R⊛

to say
dire
DEE-Rě

to see
vedere
Vě-Dě-Rě

to sell
vendere
Věn-Dě-Rě

to send
inviare
ĒN-Vēē-ah-Rě

to show
mostrare
MŌS-TRah-Rě

to sign
firmare
FēR-Mah-Rě

to sing
cantare
Kah-Tah-Rě

to sit
sedere
Sě-Dě-Rě

to sleep
dormire
DŌR-MēE-Rě

to smile
sorridere
SŌR-Rēē-Dě-Rě

to smoke
fumare
Foo-Mah-Rě

to speak
parlare
Pah-Rh-Lah-Rě

to spell
scrivere
SKRēē-Vě-Rě

to spend
passare
Pah-S-Sah-Rě

to start / begin

iniziare

EE-NEE-TSah-REe

to stay

stare

STah-REe

to stop

fermare

FEe-R-Mah-REe

to study

studiare

SToo-DEE-ah-REe

to succeed

succedere

Soo-CHEe-DEe-REe

to swim

nuotare

NWO-Tah-REe

to take

prendere

PREeN-DEe-REe

to talk

parlare

Pah-R-Lah-REe

to teach

insegnare

EEN-SEeN-Yah-REe

to think

pensare

PEeN-Sah-REe

to tell

dire

DEE-REe

to touch

toccare

TOK-Kah-REe

to travel

viaggiare

VEE-ah-J-Jah-REe

to try

provare

PRO-Vah-REe

to turn
voltare
VOL-Tah-Re

to understand
capire
Kah-PEE-Re

to use
usare
oo-Zah-Re

to visit
visitare
VEE-ZEE-Tah-Re

to wait
aspettare
ahS-PET-Tah-Re

to walk
camminare
KahM-MEE-Nah-Re

to want
volere
VO-Le-Re

to warn
avvertire
ahV-VeR-TEE-Re

to wash
lavare
Lah-Vah-Re

to watch
guardare
GWahR-Dah-Re

to win
vincere
VEEN-CHe-Re

to work
lavorare
La-VO-Rah-Re

to worry
preoccupare
PRe-OK-Koo-Pah-Re

to write
scrivere
SKREE-Ve-Re

DICTIONARY

Each English entry is followed by the Italian word and then the EPLS Vowel Symbol System. Gender of nouns and adjectives is indicated by (m) for masculine and (f) for feminine.

A

a / an un / uno ⓞN / ⓞ-Nⓞ

a lot molto MⓞL-Tⓞ

able (to be) potere Pⓞ-Tⓔ-Rⓔ

above sopra Sⓞ-PRⓐ

accident incidente ⓔN-CHⒺ-DⒺN-Tⓔ

accommodation sistemazione

   SⒺS-Tⓔ-Mⓐ-TSⒺ-Ⓞ-Nⓔ

account conto KⓞN-Tⓞ

address indirizzo ⓔN-DⒺ-RⒺT-TSⓞ

admission ingresso ⓔN-GRⓔS-Sⓞ

afraid (to be) aver paura

   ⓐ-VⓔR Pⓐ-ⓞ-Rⓐ

after dopo Dⓞ-Pⓞ

afternoon pomeriggio Pⓞ-Mⓔ-RⒺ-Jⓞ

air conditioning aria condizionata

   ⓐ-RⒺ-ⓐ KⓞN-DⒺ-TSⒺ-Ⓞ-Nⓐ-Tⓐ

---

aircraft aereo ah-é-Ré-O

airline compagnia aerea

   KOM-Pah-NEE-ah ah-é-Ré-ah

airport aeroporto ah-é-RO-POR-TO

aisle corridoio KO-REE-DO-EE-O

all tutto TOOT-TO

almost quasi KWah-ZEE

alone solo SO-LO

also anche ahN-Ké

always sempre SéM-PRé

ambulance ambulanza ahM-Boo-Lah-N-TSah

America america ah-Mé-REE-Kah

American americano ah-Mé-REE-Kah-NO

   americana ah-Mé-REE-Kah-Nah

and e é

another un altro ooN ahL-TRO

anything qualsiasi cosa

   KWahL-SEE-ah-SEE KO-Sah

apartment appartamento

   ahP-Pah-Tah-MéN-TO

appetizers antipasti ahN-TEE-Pah-S-TEE

apple mela Mé-Lah

appointment appuntamento

    (ah)P-P(oo)N-T(ah)-M(e)N-T(o)

April aprile (ah)-PR(ee)-L(e)

arrival arrivo (ah)-R(ee)-V(o)

arrive (to) arrivare (ah)-R(ee)-V(ah)-R(e)

ashtray portacenere P(o)R-T(ah)-CH(e)-N(e)-R(e)

aspirin aspirina (ah)S-P(ee)-R(ee)-N(ah)

attention attenzione (ah)T-T(e)N-TS(ee)-(o)-N(e)

August agosto (ah)-G(o)S-T(o)

Australia Australia (ow)-STR(ah)-L(ee)-(ah)

Australian Australiano (m)

    (ow)-STR(ah)-L(ee)-(ah)-N(o)

    Australiana (f) (ow)-STR(ah)-L(ee)-(ah)-N(ah)

author autore (ow)-T(o)-R(e)

automobile macchina M(ah)-K(ee)-N(ah)

autumn autunno (ow)-T(oo)N-N(o)

avenue corso K(o)R-S(o)

awful terribile T(e)-R(ee)-B(ee)-L(e)

B

baby bambino B(ah)M-B(ee)-N(o)

babysitter babysitter B(e)-B(ee)-S(ee)-T(e)R

bacon pancetta P(ah)N-CH(e)T-T(ah)

bad cattivo KⓐT-TⒺⒺ-VⓄ

bag borsa BⓄⓇB-Sⓐ

baggage bagaglio Bⓐ-Gⓐ'L-YⓄ

baked al forno ⓐL FⓄⓇB-NⓄ

bakery (bread) panetteria

　　 Pⓐ-NⒺT-TⒺ-ⓇⒺⒺ-ⓐ

banana banana Bⓐ-Nⓐ'-Nⓐ

Band-Aid cerotto CHⒺ-ⓇⓄT-TⓄ

bank banca BⓐN-Kⓐ

barbershop barbiere BⓐⓇB-BⒺⒺ-Ⓔ'-ⓇⒺ

bartender barista Bⓐ-ⓇⒺⒺS-Tⓐ

bath bagno BⓐN-YⓄ

bathing suit costume da bagno

　　 KⓄS-Tⓞⓞ-MⒺ Dⓐ BⓐN-YⓄ

bathroom bagno BⓐN-YⓄ

battery batteria Bⓐ'T-TⒺ-ⓇⒺⒺ-ⓐ

beach spiaggia SPⒺⒺ-ⓐ'-Jⓐ

beautiful bellissimo BⒺL-LⒺⒺS-SⒺⒺ-MⓄ

beauty shop salone di belleza

　　 Sⓐ-LⓄ'-NⒺ DⒺⒺ BⒺL-LⒺ'T-Sⓐ

bed letto LⒺ'T-TⓄ

beef manzo Mⓐ'N-TSⓄ

beer birra BEE-Bah

bellman fattorino Fah-T-TO-BEE-NO

belt cintura CHEEN-Too-Bah

big grande GBahN-Dë

bill conto KON-TO

black nero Në-BO

blanket coperta KO-PëB-Tah

blue blu BLoo

boat barca Bah'B-Kah

book libro LEE-BBO

bookstore libreria LEE-BBë-Bëë-ah

border confine KON-Fëë-Në

boy ragazzo Bah-Gah'T-TSO

bracelet bracciale BBah-CHEE-ah-Lë

brakes freni FBë-NEE

bread pane Pah-Në

breakfast colazione KO-Lah-TSEE-O-Në

broiled alla griglia ahL-Lah GBEEL-Yah

brown marrone Mah-BO-Në

brush spazzola SPah'T-TSO-Lah

building edificio ë-DEE-Fëë-CHO

bus autobus ow-TO-BooS

bus station stazione dell'autobus

STah-TSEE-O-NE DEL ow-TO-BooS

bus stop fermata dell'autobus

FER-Mah-Tah DEL ow-TO-BooS

business affari ahF-Fah-REE

butter burro Boo-BO

buy (to) comprare KOM-PRah-RE

C

cab tassì Tah-SEE

call (to) chiamare KEE-ah-Mah-RE

camera macchina fotografica

Mah-KEE-Nah FO-TO-GRah-FEE-Kah

Canada Canada Kah-Nah-Dah

Canadian Canadese Kah-Nah-DE-ZE

candy caramella Kah-Bah-MEL-Lah

car auto ow-TO

carrot carota Kah-BO-Tah

castle castello KahS-TEL-LO

cathedral cattedrale Kah-TE-DRah-LE

celebration celebrazione

CHE-LE-BRah-TSEE-O-NE

center centro CHEN-TRO

cereal cereali CH⊕-R⊕-⊕-L⊕

chair sedia S⊕-D⊕-⊕

champagne champagne SH⊕M-P⊕N-Y⊕

change (to) cambiare K⊕M-B⊕-⊕-R⊕

cheap a buon mercato

　　⊕ BW⊙N M⊕R-K⊕-T⊙

check (bill in a restaurant) conto K⊙N-T⊙

cheers salute S⊕-L⊚-T⊕

cheese formaggio F⊙R-M⊕-J⊙

chicken pollo P⊙L-L⊙

child bambino B⊕M-B⊕-N⊙

chocolate (flavor) cioccolata

　　CH⊙K-K⊙-L⊕-T⊕

church chiesa K⊕-⊕-S⊕

cigar sigaro S⊕-G⊕-R⊙

cigarettes sigarette S⊕-G⊕-R⊕T-T⊕

city città CH⊕T-T⊕

clean pulito P⊚-L⊕-T⊙

close (to) chiudere K⊕-⊚-D⊕-R⊕

closed chiuso KY⊚-Z⊙

clothes vestiti V⊕S-T⊕-T⊕

cocktail cocktail K⊙K-T⊕L

coffee caffé KÄH-FÉ

cold (temperature) freddo FRÉD-DO

comb pettine PÉT-TÉE-NÉ

come (to) venire VÉ-NÉE-RÉ

company (business) ditta DÉET-TÄH

computer computer KOM-PYÖÖ-TÉR

concert concerto KON-CHÉR-TO

condom preservativo

   PRÉ-SÉR-VÄH-TÉE-VO

conference conferenza

   KON-FÉ-RÉN-TSÄH

conference room sala conferenze

   SÄH-LÄH KON-FÉ-RÉN-TSÉ

congratulations congratulazioni

   KON-GRÄH-TÖÖ-LÄH-TSÉE-Ó-NÉE

copy machine fotocopiatrice

   FO-TO-KO-PÉE-äh-TRÉE-CHÉ

corn granturco GRÄHN-TÖÖR-KO

cough medicine sciroppo per la tosse

   SHÉER-ÓP-PO PÉR LÄH TÓS-SÉ

cover charge coperto KO-PÉR-TO

crab granchio GRÄHN-KÉE-O

cream crema KRĒ-Mah

credit card carta di credito

   KahR-Tah DĒ KRĒ-DĒ-TO

cup tazza Tah-TSah

customs dogana DO-Gah-Nah

D

dance (to) ballare Bah-L-Lah-RĒ

dangerous pericoloso PĒ-RĒ-KO-LO-SO

date (calendar) data Dah-Tah

day giorno JĒ-OR-NO

December dicembre DĒ-CHĒM-BRĒ

delicious delizioso DĒ-LĒ-TSĒ-O-SO

delighted lietissimo LĒ-Ē-TĒ-SĒ-MO

dentist dentista DĒN-TĒS-Tah

deodorant deodorante DĒ-O-DO-Rah-N-TĒ

department store grande magazzino

   GRah-N-DĒ Mah-Gah-TSĒ-NO

departure partenza Pah-R-TĒN-TSah

dessert dolce DOL-CHĒ

detour deviazione DĒ-VĒ-ah-TSĒ-O-NĒ

diabetic diabetico DĒ-ah-BĒ-TĒ-KO

diarrhea diarrea DĒ-ah-RĒ-ah

dictionary dizionario DEE-TSEE-O-Nah-REE-O

dinner cena CHE-Nah

dining room sala da pranzo

   Sah-Lah Dah PRah-TSO

directions indicazioni

   EEN-DEE-Kah-TSEE-O-NEE

dirty sporco SPOR-KO

disabled invalido EEN-Vah-LEE-DO

discount sconto SKON-TO

distance distanza DEES-Tah-TSah

doctor dottore DOT-TO-REE

document documento DO-Koo-MEN-TO

dollar dollaro DOL-Lah-RO

down giú Joo

downtown in centro EEN CHEN-TRO

dress vestito VES-TEE-TO

drink (to) bere BE-RE

drive (to) guidare GWEE-Dah-RE

drugstore farmacia FahR-Mah-CHEE-ah

dry cleaner lavanderia a secco

   Lah-Vah-N-DE-REE-ah ah SEK-KO

duck anitra ah-NEE-TRah

E

ear orecchio Ⓞ-Rⓔ-Kⓔ-Ⓞ

ear drops gocce per le orecchie

GⓄ-CHⓔ Pⓔⓡ Lⓔ Ⓞ-Rⓔ-Kⓔ-ⓔ

early presto PRⓔS-TⓄ

east est ⓔST

easy facile Fⓐ-CHⓔ-Lⓔ

eat (to) mangiare MⓐN-Jⓐ-Rⓔ

eggs (fried) uova fritte WⓄ-Vⓐ FRⓔT-TⓄ

eggs (scrambled) uova strapazzate

WⓄ-Vⓐ STRⓐ-Pⓐ-TSⓐ-Tⓔ

eggs uova WⓄ-Vⓐ

electricity corrente KⓄ-RⓔN-Tⓔ

elevator ascensore ⓐ-SHⓔN-SⓄ-Rⓔ

embassy ambasciata ⓐM-Bⓐ-SHⓐ-Tⓐ

emergency emergenza ⓔ-MⓔR-JⓔN-TSⓐ

England Inghilteria ⓔN-GⓔL-TⓔR-ⓔ-ⓤ

English inglese ⓔN-GLⓔ-Zⓔ

enough basta BⓐS-Tⓐ

entrance ingresso ⓔN-GRⓔS-SⓄ

envelope busta BⓄⓄS-Tⓐ

evening sera SĔ́-Ɓah

everything tutto TOOT-TO

excellent eccellente Ĕ-CHĔL-LĔN-TĔ

excuse me mi scusi MEE SKOO-ZEE

exit uscita OO-SHĔ́-Tah

expensive caro Kah́-ƁO

eyedrops gocce per gli occhi

GO-CHĔ PĔƁ LYĔ OK-KĔ

eyes occhi OK-KĔ

F

face faccia Fah́-CHah

far lontano LON-Tah-NO

fare (cost) costo KO S-TO

fast veloce VĔ-LO-CHĔ

fax machine macchina per fax

Mah́K-KĔ-Nah PĔƁ FahKS

February febbraio FĔB-BƁah́-YO

few alcuni ahL-KOO-NĔ

film (movie) rull ƁOOL

film (camera) rullino ƁOOL-LĔ-NO

fine (very well) bene BĔ́-NĔ

finger dito Dî-T⓯

fire extinguisher estintore ⓯S-T⓮N-T⓯-Rⓩ

fire fuoco FW⓯-K⓯

first primo PR⓮-M⓯

fish pesce Pⓩ-SHⓩ

flight volo V⓯-L⓯

florist shop fiorista F⓮-⓯-R⓮S-TⒶ

flower fiore F⓮-⓯-Rⓩ

food cibo CH⓮-B⓯

foot piede P⓮-ⓩ-Dⓩ

fork forchetta F⓯R-KⓩT-TⒶ

french fries patatine fritte

   PⒶ-TⒶ-T⓮-Nⓩ   FR⓮T-Tⓩ

fresh fresco FRⓩS-K⓯

Friday venerdì Vⓩ-NⓩR-D⓮

fried fritto FR⓮T-T⓯

friend amico ⒶM-⓮-K⓯

fruit frutta FR⓬T-TⒶ

funny divertente D⓮-VⓩR-TⓩN-Tⓩ

G

gas station distributore

   DⓩS-TR⓮-B⓬-T⓯-Rⓩ

gasoline benzina BEN-TSEE-Nah

gate cancello KahN-CHEL-LO

gentleman signore SEEN-YO-RE

gift regalo RE-Gah-LO

girl ragazza Rah-GahT-TSah

glass (drinking) bicchiere BEEK-YE-RE

glasses (eye) occhiali OK-KEE-ah-LEE

gloves guanti GWahN-TEE

go forza FOR-TSah

gold oro O-RO

golf course campo di golf

KahM-PO DEE GOLF

golf golf GOLF

good buono BWO-NO

good-bye arrivederci ah-REE-VE-DER-CHEE

goose oca O-Kah

grapes uva OO-Vah

grateful grato GRah-TO

gray grigio GREE-JO

green verde VER-DE

grocery store drogheria DRO-GE-REE-ah

group gruppo GROOP-PO

guide guida GWEE-Dah

H

hair capelli Kah-PEL-LEE

hairbrush spazzola SPah-TSO-Lah

haircut taglio di capelli

    TahL-YO DEE Kah-PEL-LEE

ham prosciutto PRO-SHOOT-TO

hamburger hamburger ahM-BOOR-GER

hand mano Mah-NO

happy felice / contento

    FE-LEE-CHE / KON-TEN-TO

have (I) ho O

he lui LOO-EE

head testa TES-Tah

headache mal di testa MahL DEE TES-Tah

health club club ginnico KLOOB JEEN-NEE-KO

heart cuore KWO-RE

heart condition debole di cuore

    DE-BO-LE DEE KWO-RE

heat calore Kah-LO-RE

hello ciao CHow

help aiuto ah-YOO-TO

here qui KWEE

holiday vacanza Vah-Kah'N-Zah

hospital ospedale OS-PE-Dah-LE

hot dog hot dog ahT DahG

hotel hotel O-TEL

hour ora O'-Rah

how come KO'-ME

hurry up sbrigarsi ZBREE-Gah'R-SEE

I

I io EE'-O

ice ghiaccio GEE-ah-CHO

ice cream gelato JE-Lah-TO

ice cubes cubetti di ghiaccio
    KOO-BET-TEE DEE GEE-ah-CHO

ill ammalato ahM-Mah-Lah-TO

important importante EEM-POR-Tah'N-TE

indigestion indigestione
    EEN-DEE-JES-TEE-O'-NE

information informazione
    EEN-FOR-Mah-TSEE-O'-NE

inn albergo (ah)L-B(eh)R-G(o)

interpreter interprete (ee)N-T(eh)R-PR(eh)-T(eh)

Italian italiano (ee)-T(ah)-L(ee)-(ah)-N(o)

Italy lingua italiana

L(ee)N-GW(uh) (ee)-T(ah)-L(ee)-(ah)-N(ah)

Italy Italia (ee)-T(ah)-L(ee)-(ah)

J

jacket giubbotto J(oo)-B(o)T-T(o)

jam marmellata M(ah)R-M(eh)L-L(ah)-T(ah)

January gennaio J(eh)N-N(ah)-Y(o)

jewelry gioielli J(o)-Y(eh)L-L(ee)

jewelry store gioielleria J(o)-Y(eh)L-L(o)-R(ee)-(ah)

job lavoro L(ah)-V(o)-R(o)

juice succo S(oo)K-K(o)

June giugno J(oo)N-Y(o)

July luglio L(oo)L-Y(o)

K

ketchup ketchup K(eh)-CH(oo)P

key chiave K(ee)-(ah)-V(eh)

kiss bacio B(ah)-CH(o)

knife coltello K(o)L-T(eh)L-L(o)

know (to) sapere S(ah)-P(eh)-R(eh)

L

ladies' restroom toilette per le donne
TWah-LĔT PĔR LĔ DŌN-NĔ

lady signora SĒN-YŌ-Bah

lamb agnello ahN-YĔL-LŌ

language lingua LĒN-GWah

large grande GBahN-DĔ

late tardi TahB-DĒ

laundry lavanderia Lah-VahN-DĔ-BĒ-ah

lawyer avvocato ahV-VŌ-Kah-TŌ

left (direction) sinistra SĒ-NĒS-TBah

leg gamba GahM-Bah

lemon limone LĒ-MŌ-NĔ

less meno MĔ-NŌ

letter lettera LĔT-TĔ-Bah

lettuce lattuga Lah-Tōō-Gah

light luce Lōō-CHĔ

like (to) piacere PĒ-ah-CHĔ-BĔ

like (I would) vorrei VŌ-BĔ-Ē

lip labbro LahB-BBŌ

lipstick rossetto BŌS-SĔT-TŌ

little piccolo PEEK-KO-LO

little poco PO-KO

live (to) vivere VEE-Vê-Rê

lobster aragosta ah-Rah-GOS-Tah

long lungo LOON-GO

lost perduto PêR-DOO-TO

love amore ah-MO-Rê

luck fortuna FOR-TOO-Nah

luggage bagaglio Bah-Gah'L-YO

lunch pranzo PRahN-TSO

M

maid cameriera Kah-Mê-Rêê-ê-Rah

mail posta POS-Tah

makeup trucco TROOK-KO

man uomo WO-MO

manager direttore DEE-RêT-TO-Rê

map cartina KahR-Têê-Nah

March marzo MahR-TSO

market mercato MêR-Kah-TO

matches fiammiferi FEE-ahM-MEE-Fê-REE

May maggio Mah-JO

mayonnaise maionese Mah-YO-NÊ-SÊ

meal pasto Pah'S-TO

meat carne Kah'B-NÊ

mechanic meccanico MÊK-Kah'-NÊ-KO

medicine medicina MÊ-DÊ-CHÊ-Nah

meeting incontro ÊN-KO'N-TBO

mens' restroom toilette per uomini
    TWah-LÊ'T PÊB WO-MÊ-NÊ

menu menù MÊ-Noo'

message messaggio MÊS-Sah'-JO

milk latte Lah'T-TÊ

mineral water acqua minerale ah-KWah
    MÊ-NÊ-Bah'-LÊ

minute minuto MÊ-Noo'-TO

Miss Signorina SÊN-YO-BÊ'-Nah

mistake sbaglio TSBah'L-YO

misunderstood frainteso
    FBah-ÊN-TÊ'-ZO

moment momento MO-MÊ'N-TO

Monday lunedì Loo-NÊ-DÊ'

money soldi SO'L-DÊ

month mese MÊ'-SÊ

monument monumento MO-Noo-MĔN-TO

more piú PĔE-oo

morning mattina Mah-T-TĔE-Nah

mosque moschea MOS-KĔ-ah

mother madre Mah-DRĔ

mountain montagna MON-Tah-N-Yah

movies film FĔELM

Mr. Signore SĔEN-YO-RĔ

Mrs. Signora SĔEN-YO-Rah

much, too molto MOL-TO

museum museo Moo-SĔ-O

mushrooms funghi Foon-GĔE

music musica Moo-SĔE-Kah

mustard senape SĔ-Nah-PĔ

N

nail polish smalto per le unghie

   SMah L-TO PĔR LĔ oon-GĔE-Ĕ

name nome NO-MĔ

napkin tovagliolo TO-Vah L-YO-LO

near vicino VĔE-CHĔE-NO

neck collo KOL-LO

need (I) ho bisogno ` Ⓞ BⒺⒺ-ZⓄN-YⓄ

never mai MⓐⒽ-ⒺⒺ

newspaper giornale JⓄR-NⓐⒽ-LⒺ

news stand edicola Ⓔ-DⒺⒺ-KⓄ-LⓐⒽ

next time la prossima volta

    LⓐⒽ PRⓄS-SⒺⒺ-MⓐⒽ VⓄL-TⓐⒽ

night notte NⓄT-TⒺ

nightclub locale notturno

    LⓄ-KⓐⒽ-LⒺ NⓄT-TⓄⓄR-NⓄ

no no NⓄ

no smoking non fumatori

    NⓄN FⓄⓄ-MⓐⒽ-TⓄ-RⒺⒺ

noon mezzogiorno MⒺ-TSⓄ-JⓄR-NⓄ

north nord NⓄRD

notary notaio NⓄ-TⓐⒽ-YⓄ

November novembre NⓄ-VⒺM-BRⒺ

now adesso ⓐⒽ-DⒺS-SⓄ

number numero NⓄⓄ-MⒺ-RⓄ

nurse infermiera ⒺN-FⒺR-MⒺⒺ-Ⓔ-RⓐⒽ

O

occupied occupato ⓄK-KⓄⓄ-PⓐⒽ-TⓄ

ocean oceano Ⓞ-CHⒺ-ⓐⒽ-NⓄ

October ottobre ⓄT-TⓄ-BRⒺ

officer ufficiale ⓄⓄF-FⒺⒺ-CHⓐⒽ-LⒺ

oil olio ⓄL-YⓄ

omelet frittata FRⒺⒺT-TⓐⒽ-TⓐⒽ

one-way (traffic) senso unico

    SⒺN-SⓄ ⓄⓄ-NⒺⒺ-KⓄ

onions cipolle CHⒺⒺ-PⓄLˊ-LⒺ

open (to) aprire ⓐⒽ-PRⒺⒺ-RⒺ

opera opera Ⓞˊ-PⒺ-RⓐⒽ

operator centralinista

    CHⒺN-TRⓐⒽ-LⒺⒺ-NⒺⒺˊS-TⓐⒽ

optician ottico ⓄT-TⒺⒺˊ-KⓄ

orange arancione ⓐⒽ-RⓐⒽN-CHⓄˊ-NⒶ

orange (fruit) arancia ⓐⒽ-RⓐⒽN-CHⓐⒽ

order (to) ordinare ⓄR-DⒺⒺ-NⓐⒽ-RⒺ

original originale Ⓞ-RⒺⒺ-JⒺⒺ-NⓐⒽˊ-LⒺ

owner proprietario PRⓄ-PRⒺⒺ-Ⓔˊ-TⓐⒽ-RⒺⒺˊ-Ⓞ

oyster ostriche ⓄˊS-TRⒺⒺ-KⒺ

P

package pacco PⓐⒾK-KⓄ

paid pagato PⓐⒽ-GⓐⒽˊ-TⓄ

pain dolore DⓄ-LⓄˊ-RⒺ

painting dipinto DEE-PEEN-TO

pantyhose collant KOL-LahNT

paper carta KahB-Tah

park (to) parcheggiare PahB-KEE-JahB-BEE

park parco PahB-KO

partner (business) socio SO-CHEE-O

party festa FEES-Tah

passenger passeggero PahS-SEE-JEE-BO

passport passaporto PahS-Sah-POB-TO

pasta pasta PahS-Tah

pastry shop pasticcini PahS-TEE-CHEE-NEE

pen penna PEEN-Nah

pencil matita Mah-TEE-Tah

pepper pepe PEE-PEE

perfume profumo PBO-Foo-MO

person persona PEEB-SO-Nah

person to person diretta con preavviso
   DEE-BEET-Tah KON PBEE-ah-VEE-ZO

pharmacist un farmacista
   ooN FahB-Mah-CHEES-Tah

pharmacy farmacia FahB-Mah-CHEE-ah

phone book elenco telefonica

ⓔ-LⓔN-KⓄ Tⓔ-Lⓔ-FⓄ-Nⓔⓔ-Kⓐⓗ

photo foto FⓄ-TⓄ

photographer fotografo FⓄ-TⓄ-GRⓐⓗ-FⓄ

pie, cake torta TⓄR-Tⓐⓗ

pillow cuscino Kⓞⓞ-SHⓔⓔ-NⓄ

pink rosa RⓄ-Zⓐⓗ

pizza pizza PⓔⓔT-Sⓐⓗ

plastic plastica PLⓐⓗS-Tⓔⓔ-Kⓐⓗ

plate piatto Pⓔⓔ-ⓐⓗT-TⓄ

please per favore / per piacere

PⓔR Fⓐⓗ-VⓄ-Rⓔ / PⓔR Pⓔⓔ-ⓐⓗ-CHⓔ-Rⓔ

pleasure piacere Pⓔⓔ-ⓐⓗ-CHⓔ-Rⓔ

police polizia PⓄ-Lⓔⓔ-TSⓔⓔ-ⓐⓗ

police station stazione di polizia

STⓐⓗ-TSⓔⓔ-Ⓞ-Nⓔ Dⓔⓔ PⓄ-Lⓔⓔ-TSⓔⓔ-ⓐⓗ

pork maiale Mⓐⓗ-Yⓐⓗ-Lⓔ

porter facchino Fⓐⓗ-Kⓔⓔ-NⓄ

post office ufficio postale

ⓞⓞ-Fⓔⓔ-CHⓄ PⓄS-Tⓐⓗ-Lⓔ

postcard cartolina KⓐⓗR-TⓄ-Lⓔⓔ-Nⓐⓗ

potato patata Pⓐⓗ-Tⓐⓗ-Tⓐⓗ

pregnant incinta ĒN-CHĒN-Tah

prescription ricetta RĒ-CHĒT-Tah

price prezzo PRĒ-TSO

problem problema PRO-BLĒ-Mah

profession professione

PRO-FĒS-SĒ-O-NĒ

public pubblico POOB-BLĒ-KO

public telephone telefono pubblico

TĒ-LĒ-FO-NO POOB-BLĒ-KO

purified purificata POO-RĒ-FĒ-Kah-Tah

purple porpora POR-PO-Rah

purse borsetta BOR-SĒT-Tah

Q

quality qualità KWah-LĒ-Tah

question domanda DO-Mah-N-Dah

quickly presto / subito

PRĒS-TO / SOO-BĒ-TO

quiet! quieto! KWĒ-Ē-TO

quiet (to be) zitto TSĒT-TO

R

radio radio Rah-DĒ-O

railroad ferrovia FⒺB-Ⓞ-VⒺ-ⓐⓗ

rain pioggia PⒺ-Ⓞ-Jⓐⓗ

raincoat impermeabile

ⒺM-PⒺB-MⒺ-ⓐⓗ-BⒺ-LⒺ

ramp rampa BⓐⓗM-Pⓐⓗ

rare (steak) al sangue ⓐⓗL SⓐⓗN-GWⒺ

razor blades lamette Lⓐⓗ-MⒺT-TⒺ

ready pronto PBⓄN-TⓄ

receipt ricevuta BⒺ-CHⒺ-VⓄⓄ-Tⓐⓗ

recommend (to) raccomandare

BⓐⓗK-KⓄ-MⓐⓗN-Dⓐⓗ-BⒺ

red rosso BⓄS-SⓄ

repeat ripeta BⒺ-PⒺ-Tⓐⓗ

reservation prenotazione

PBⒺ-NⓄ-Tⓐⓗ-TSⒺ-Ⓞ-NⒺ

restaurant ristorante BⒺS-TⓄ-BⓐⓗN-TⒺ

return (to come back) ritornare

BⒺ-TⓄB-Nⓐⓗ-BⒺ

return (to give back) restituire

BⒺS-TⒺ-TⓄⓄ-Ⓔ-BⒺ

rice riso BⒺ-ZⓄ

rich ricco BⒺK-KⓄ

right (correct) giusto J@S-T@

right (direction) destra D@S-TR@

road strada STR@-D@

room stanza ST@N-TS@

round trip andata e ritorno

    @N-D@-T@ @ R@-T@R-N@

S

safe (box) cassaforte K@S-S@-F@R-T@

salad insalata @N-S@-L@-T@

sale vendita V@N-D@-T@

salmon salmone S@L-M@N-@

salt sale S@-L@

sandwich panino P@-N@-N@

Saturday sabato S@-B@-T@

scissors forbici F@R-B@-CH@

sculpture scultura SK@L-T@-R@

seafood frutti di mare

    FR@-T@ D@ M@-R@

season stagione ST@-J@-N@

seat posto P@S-T@

secretary segretario S@G-R@-T@R-Y@

section sezione S@-TS@-@-N@

September settembre SĔT-TĔM-BRĕ

service servizio SĔR-VĒ-TSĒ-O

several diversi DĒ-VĔR-SĒ

shampoo shampoo SHäM-PO

sheets (bed) lenzuola LĔN-TSWO-Läh

shirt camicia Käh-MĒ-CHäh

shoe scarpa SKäR-Päh

shoe store negozio di scarpe

    NĔ-GO-TSĒ-O DĒ SKäRP-Pĕ

shop (store) negozio NĔ-GO-TSĒ-O

shopping center centro commerciale

    CHĔN-TRO KO-MĔR-CHĒ-äh-Lĕ

shower doccia DO-CHäh

shrimp gamberetti GähM-BĔ-RĔT-TĒ

sick malato Mäh-Läh-TO

sign (display) cartello KäR-TĔL-LO

signature firma FĒR-Mäh

single singolo SĒN-GO-LO

sir signore SĒN-YO-Rĕ

sister sorella SO-RĔL-Läh

size taglia TäL-Yäh

skin pelle PĔL-Lĕ

skirt gonna GÓN-N@h

sleeve manica M@hN-N©-K@h

slowly lentamente L©N-T@h-M©N-T©

small piccolo P©K-K©-LO

smile (to) sorridere S©R-R©-D©-R©

smoke (to) fumare F©-M@h-R©

soap sapone S@h-PÓN-©

sock calza K@hL-TS@h

some qualche KW@hL-K©

something qualcosa KW@hL-K©-Z@h

sometimes a volta @h VÓL-T@h

soon presto PR©S-T©

sorry (I am) mi dispiace

   M© D©S-P©-@h-CH©

soup minestra M©-N©S-TR@h

south sud S©D

souvenir ricordo R©-KÓR-D©

speciality specialità SP©-CH©-@h-L©-T@h

speed velocità V©-L©-CH©-T@h

spoon cucchiaio K©K-Y@h-Y©

sport sport SP©RT

spring primavera PR©-M@h-V©-R@h

stairs scale SKah-Lē

stamp francobollo FRahN-KO-BOL-LO

station stazione STah-TSEE-O-Nē

steak bistecca BEES-Tē-Kah

steamed al vapore ahL Vah-PO-Rē

stop! si fermi! SEE Fē-BEB-MEE

store negozio Nē-GO-TSEE-O

storm temporale Tē-M-PO-Rah-Lē

straight ahead avanti diritto

　　　ah-VahN-TEE DEE-REET-TO

strawberry fragola FRah-GO-Lah

street via VEE-ah

string corda KOB-Dah

subway metropolitana

　　　Mē-TRO-PO-LEE-Tah-Nah

sugar zucchero TSOOK-Kē-BO

suit (clothes) abito completo

　　　ah-BEE-TO KOM-PLē-TO

suitcase valigia Vah-Lē-Jah

summer estate ēS-Tah-Tē

sun sole SO-Lē

Sunday domenica DO-Mē-NEE-Kah

sunglasses occhiali da sole

OK-KEE-ah-LEE Dah SO-LE

suntan lotion crema solare

KREH-Mah SO-Lah-REH

supermarket supermercato

SOO-PER-MER-Kah-TO

surprise sorpresa SOR-PREH-Zah

sweet dolce DOL-CHE

swim (to) nuotare NWO-Tah-REH

swimming pool piscina PEE-SHEE-Nah

synagogue sinagoga SEE-Nah-GO-Gah

T

table tavola Tah-VO-Lah

tampons tamponi TahM-PO-NEE

tape (sticky) nastro adesivo

Nah'S-TRO ah-DEH-SEE-VO

tape recorder registratore

REH-JEE-STRah-TO-REH

tax imposta EEM-POS-Tah

taxi tassì Tah-SEE

tea tè TE

telephone telefono TE-LE-FO-NO

television televisione TĔ-LĔ-VĒ-SĒ-Ō-NĔ

temperature temperatura TĔM-PĔR-ah-TOO-Rah

temple tempio TĔM-PĒ-Ō

tennis tennis TĔN-NĒS

tennis court campo da tennis

    KahM-PŌ Dah TĔN-NĒS

thank you molte grazie

    MŌL-TĔ GRah-TSĒ-Ĕ

that quello KWĔL-LŌ

the il / la / lo / l' / i / gli / le

    ĒL / Lah / LŌ / L / Ē / LYĒ / LĔ

theater teatro TĔ-ah-TRŌ

there là Lah

they loro LŌ-RŌ

this questo KWĔS-TŌ

thread filo FĒ-LŌ

throat gola GŌ-Lah

Thursday giovedì JŌ-VĔ-DĒ

ticket biglietto BĒL-YĔ-TŌ

tie cravatta KRah-VahT-Tah

time ora Ō-Rah

tip (gratuity) mancia MahN-CHah

tire gomma GOM-Mah

tired stanco STahN-KO

toast pane tostato Pah-Nê TOS-Tah-TO

tobacco tabacco Tah-BahK-KO

today oggi O-JEE

toe dito del piede DEE-TO DêL PEE-ê-Dê

together insieme EEN-SEE-ê-Mê

toilet toilette / gabinetto
    TWah-LêT / Gah-BEE-NêT-TO

toilet paper carta igienica
    KahR-Tah EE-Jê-NEE-Kah

tomato pomodoro PO-MO-DO-RO

tomorrow domani DO-Mah-NEE

tooth ache mal di denti
    MahL DEE DêN-TEE

toothbrush spazzolino da denti
    SPahT-TSO-LEE-NO Dah DêN-TEE

toothpaste dentifricio DêN-TEE-FRêê-CHO

toothpick stuzzicadenti
    STOO-TSEE-Kah-DêN-TEE

tour giro JEE-RO

tourist turista TOO-REES-Tah

tourist office ufficio del turismo

O-FEE-CHO DEL TOO-REES-MO

towel asciugamano ah-SHOO-GAH-MAH-NO

train treno TREH-NO

travel agency agenzia di viaggio

ah-JEN-TSEE-Yah DEE VEE-ah-JO

traveler's check traveler's check

TRAH-VEL-ERS CHEK

trip viaggio VEE-ah-JO

trousers pantaloni PahN-Tah-LO-NEE

trout trota TRO-Tah

truth verità VEH-REE-Tah

Tuesday martedì MahR-TEH-DEE

turkey tacchino Tah-KEE-NO

U

umbrella ombrello OM-BREL-LO

understand (to) capire Kah-PEE-REH

underwear mutande MOO-TahN-DEH

United Kingdom Regno Unito

REH-NYO OO-NEE-TO

United States Stati Uniti STah-TEE OO-NEE-TEE

university università ⊚-N◉-V◉R-S◉-T◎

up su S⊚

urgent urgente ⊚R-J◉N-T◉

V

vacancies (accommodation) stanze libere
ST◎N-TS◉ L◉-B◉-R◉

vacant libero L◉-B◉-R◎

vacation vacanza V◎-K◎N-TS◎

valuable di valore D◉ V◎-L◎-R◉

value valore V◎-L◎-R◉

vanilla vaniglia V◎-N◉L-Y◎

veal vitello V◉-T◉L-L◎

vegetables verdure V◉R-D◎-R◉

view vista V◉S-T◎

vinegar aceto ◎-CH◉-T◎

voyage viaggio V◉-◎-J◎

W

wait aspetta ◎-SP◉T-◎

waiter cameriere K◎-M◉-R◉-◉-R◉

waitress cameriera K◎-M◉-R◉-◉-R◎

want (I) voglio V◎L-Y◎

wash (to) lavare L◎-V◎-R◉

watch orologio Ⓞ-ⓇⓄ-LⓄ-JⓄ

watch out attenzione ⓐⓗT-Tⓔ N-TSⓔ Ⓔ-Ⓞ-Nⓔ

water acqua ⓐⓗ-KWⓐⓗ

water (drinking) acqua potabile

　ⓐⓗ-KWⓐⓗ PⓄ-Tⓐⓗ-Bⓔ Ⓔ-Lⓔ

we noi NⓄⓥ

weather tempo Tⓔ M-PⓄ

Wednesday mercoledì Mⓔ Ⓡ-KⓄ-Lⓔ-Dⓔ Ⓔ

week settimana Sⓔ T-Tⓔ Ⓔ-Mⓐⓗ-Nⓐⓗ

weekend fine settimana

　Fⓔ Ⓔ-Nⓔ Sⓔ T-Tⓔ Ⓔ-Mⓐⓗ-Nⓐⓗ

welcome benvenuto Bⓔ N-Vⓔ-NⓄ Ⓞ-TⓄ

well done ben cotto Bⓔ N KⓄ-TⓄ

west ovest Ⓞ-Vⓔ ST

what cosa KⓄ-Zⓐⓗ

wheelchair sedia a rotelle

　Sⓔ D-Yⓐⓗ ⓐⓗ ⓇⓄ-Tⓔ L-Lⓔ

when? quando? KWⓐⓗN-DⓄ

where? dove? DⓄ-Vⓔ

which? quale? KWⓐⓗ-Lⓔ

white bianco Bⓔ Ⓔ-ⓐⓗN-KⓄ

who? chi? Kⓔ Ⓔ

why? perché? PĚR-KĒ

wife moglie MŌL-YĚ

wind vento VĚN-TŌ

window finestra FĒ-NĚS-TRah

wine vino VĒ-NŌ

wine list lista dei vini LĒS-Tah DĚ VĒ-NĒ

winter inverno ĒN-VĚR-NŌ

with con KŌN

woman donna DŌN-Nah

wonderful meraviglioso
   MĚ-Rah-VĒL-YŌ-SŌ

world mondo MŌN-DŌ

wrong (incorrect) bagliato ZBah-Yah-TŌ

XYZ

year anno ahN-NO

yellow giallo Jah L-LŌ

yes sì SĒ

yesterday ieri YĚ-RĒ

you tu Too

zipper cerniera CHĚR-NĒ-Ě-Rah

zoo zoo TSŌ-O

EASILY PRONOUNCED LANGUAGE SYSTEMS

Author Clyde Peters graduated from Radford High School and the University of Hawaii and has traveled the world as a travel writer. His innovative Say It Right phrase books have revolutionized the way languages are taught and learned. Mr. Peters invented the Vowel Symbol System for easy and correct pronunciation of virtually any language. He currently continues traveling the world working on new languages and divides his spare time between Las Vegas, Nevada, and Hawaii.

Betty Chapman is a successful business woman who along with Mr. Peters founded Easily Pronounced Language Systems to promote education, travel, and custom tailored language solutions. "Moving beyond expectation to acquisition and accomplishment is possible with EPLS."

Priscilla Leal Bailey is the senior series editor for all Say It Right products and has proved indispensable in editing and implementing the EPLS Vowel Symbol System. We are forever grateful for her belief and support.

SAY IT RIGHT SERIES
Infinite Destinations
One Pronunciation System!

Audio Editions

Say It Right App on iTunes

THANKS!

The nicest thing you can say to anyone in any language is "Thank you." Try some of these languages using the incredible EPLS Vowel Symbol System.

Arabic
SH⊚⊚-KR@N

Chinese
SH©© SH©©

French
M©R-S©©

German
D@N-K⓾

Hawaiian
M@-H@-L◎

Italian
GR@T-S©©-©

Japanese
D◎-M◎

Portuguese
◎-BR©©-G@-D◎

Russian
SP@-S©©-B@

Spanish
GR@-S©©-@S

Swahili
@-S@N-T&

Tagalog
S@-L@-M@T

INDEX

QUICK REFERENCE PAGE

Hello	**Good-bye**
Buon giorno	Arrivederci
BWON JOR-NO	ah-REE-Vè-DèR-CHEE
How are you?	**Fine / Very well**
Come sta?	Molto bene
KO-Mè STah	MOL-TO Bè-Nè
Yes	**No**
Sí	No
SEE	NO
Please	**Thank you**
Per favore	Grazie
PèR Fah-VO-Rè	GRah-TSEE-è
I would like...	**Where is...**
Vorrei...	Dov'è?
VO-Rè-EE	DO-Vè...
I don't understand.	
Non capisco!	
NON Kah-PEES-KO	
Help!	
Aiuto!	
ah-YOO-TO	